A Gift from Shamash

A Science Fiction Scenario for Mythras and Mythras Imperative

By Pete Nash

Art by Jethro Lentle, Hanna Bergström and Asa De Buck

Deck Plans by Colin Driver

Additional Material by Lawrence Whitaker and Clarence Redd

Published under license in the UK by Aeon Games Publishing

www.aeongamespublishing.co.uk

ISBN 978-1-91147-119-6

Introduction

A Gift from Shamash is a Science Fiction scenario designed to demonstrate the ability of *Mythras* to adapt to any genre. It can be used standalone with *Mythras Imperative*, or in combination with the *Firearms* rules expansion if the Games Master desires. You should also be able to easily use it with the *M-Space* Science Fiction rules (based on *Mythras Imperative*) available from Frostbyte Books. It can also be easily used as a *Luther Arkwright* scenario set in a technically adept parallel.

Set in the near future as mankind starts to explore the solar system, *A Gift from Shamash* is intended to be investigative horror mixed with hard science fiction. There are no FTL drives, no artificial gravity and no hand-held lasers. As far as the characters are aware, the only intelligent life is humanity. Inspiration stems from many sources, but mainly the movies 'Alien', 'Outland' and '2010' combined with 'The Forever War' by Joe Haldeman.

Since deep space and wreck investigation are both extremely deadly environments, character mortality may well be high. The scenario was originally designed as a single shot convention game where players would take on the roll of two characters, one of the flight crew for the starship side of things, and one marine during the boarding. Sample characters are provided at the end of the scenario, along with rules for creating UN Marines. You could easily substitute these with characters created for M-Space or of your own devising with the *Mythras Imperative*, *Mythras* and *Luther Arkwright* character creation systems.

Background

The year is 2313 and Earth is in bad shape. The collapse of Europe and the Americas in the early 21st Century, followed by worldwide revolution against technocratic feudalism, led inevitably to global war. Fortunately for humanity, conflicts between the remaining powers were conducted in terms of limited exchanges of tactical nuclear weapons and a few bio-weapons which failed to have the desired effect.

Although only a few percent of humanity died in the initial exchanges, millions more were plunged into sickness, starvation and eventual civil breakdown. The wealthy and influential were butchered in the backlash by raging populations. The few that attempted to flee to their underground bunkers or private island retreats were rooted out and publically executed. Most died in the dark, smothered when their ventilation systems were blocked or filled with burning tires and petrol.

With little civil government remaining, a handful of surviving military officers seized control of the United Nations and used it as a de-facto ruling body to unify surviving nation states. The aftermath of the collapse had altered the planet irrevocably. Despite a brief drop in temperatures due to the restricted nuclear exchange, climate change proceeded to warm the polar regions. Billions returned to burning wood and coal whilst electrical grids lay in tatters. Rainfall patterns were permanently altered as was the severity of storms; it did not take long before the entire ecosystem collapsed.

Mass migrations sparked a new wave of petty wars until the UN finally subsumed the remnant militaries and imposed a ruthless autocracy, led by a handful of demagogues and once-popular civilian industrialists. Under their control, plans were laid to establish self-supporting human colonies across the solar system to ensure the survival of the human race. Key technologies were reestablished to provide launch facilities, and the ban on nuclear propulsion was waved in the blunt realisation that the Earth's atmosphere couldn't be polluted any more than it already had been.

By the mid 21st Century the UN had brought worldwide stability—at the cost of banning many civil liberties. Education systems were unified to encourage hard sciences, under the auspices of planet-wide social indoctrination. For the large part this worked; survivors of the cataclysm still bore hatred for political corruption and economic inequality, fearing the world would destroy itself if people were allowed to resort to cultural tribalism.

Nearly a century after the collapse most of the planet's hi-tech industry was in orbit, with the first colonisation attempts starting on the Moon, Mars, and several asteroids of significant size. It became obvious that technology could not offset the physiological dangers of living in space. High radiation levels and microgravity both conspired to shorten life spans and fertility to critical levels. This prompted a renaissance in bio-engineering, seeking to manipulate tolerances at the genetic level rather than overcome the technical difficulties with complex physics or improbable materials.

The maturation of the science behind the Mach-Lorenz Effect drive allowed humanity to spread to the farther limits of the solar system, establishing mining operations in Saturn's rings and the Kuiper Belt. Eventually missions were launched at the closest stars to begin surveying our nearest neighbours, using STL ships with cryogenic, torpor-induced crews travelling at low fractions of light speed.

Despite the push to explore other stars, such missions took decades and suffered high failure rates, whilst humanity had near unlimited space to disperse amongst the countless bodies of the Oort Cloud. Expansionist policies once held dear by the United Nations were instead replaced by a focus on repairing Earth's ecosystem. Its authoritarian stranglehold over humankind loosened, leading to a nostalgic return to nationalism and capitalist 'free' markets. The Earth-based UN could see which way the wind was blowing and decided to adopt a hands-off policy of supervision over a hegemony of independent, corporate colonised planetoids.

Its role in the 24th Century is now reduced to peacemaker of the solar system, being the only political entity permitted to maintain military spaceships. In

A Gift From Shamash

> **UNCC Nergal**
>
> The first of a new Tartarus class of UN customs cutters, the Nergal displaces 1,036 metric tons with a length of 63m and beam of 15m at its widest part. Propulsion is provided by twin J913D-27 ML-EM Thrusters, Chobham ceramic LiH shielding permits a top velocity of 0.14c before dangerous levels of crew irradiation, whilst outer deflection surfaces are covered by a black body ablative polymer RAM to increase thermal protection and ambient stealth, the latter further enhanced by phased directional radiators that fold out from the hull. Power is supplied via a 290MW Lerner DPF 3017HB fusion generator, backed up with a 1.2GW battery array, combined with pressurised liquid nitrogen thrusters for silent running. The class has a compliment of 15—six flight crew and a boarding section (short platoon) of nine marines.
>
> Moderately armed, weaponry incorporates a spinal mounted GSh-8-69 50mm rail cannon, twin side mounted AK-1476 35MW pulse lasers for point defense, and a dorsal located A-638 Agni-M multiple launch missile system armed with 8 anti-ship missiles (HEAP penetrator warheads). Additional defense is provided by the onboard ECM suite and one-shot decoys. Last but not least, the Nergal also possesses a ventral mounted armoured assault shuttle, capable of carrying the entire marine compliment (albeit tightly packed) over short distances, or too and from orbit.
>
> Deckplans for the UNCC Nergal and DCV Fukunusubi can be found on page 10-11. M-Space Statistics for both ships featured in this scenario can be found on page 38.

addition to maintaining law and order between the megacorps, the UN navy also tries to suppress illegal research and manufacturing that corporations would find impossible to develop on Earth. The UNSN also has a secondary, but no less important task as customs and excise officials. They ensure that nothing dangerous is brought back from the outlying stars. No intelligent life has yet been discovered; the most complex life forms have been primitive mosses and algae, which themselves pose a possible biological threat. But some scientists insist that it is only a matter of time before humanity stumbles upon other high order life.

Synopsis

The players are the crew of the **UNCC Nergal**, a navy cutter patrolling the outer reaches of the solar system. They receive an alert from a monitoring station on Triton, concerning a corporate vessel with which they have lost contact. Flight plans indicate that the ship intended to rendezvous with a minor scientific base on the moon Psamathe, in the Neptunian system (see *Mission Environs*, page 39). However it has failed to initiate deceleration procedures, leaving it on a ballistic course with no sign of slowing down from its velocity of 1% light speed.

Unresponsive to comms the silent ship is the **DCV Fukunusubi**, a deep space construction vessel which 'stumbled upon' the drifting remnants of a long overdue interstellar ship returning to Sol. What they discovered proved extremely hazardous. Members of the boarding team died investigating the drifting wreck. Others expired later when artefacts it was carrying were brought aboard. Left without flight crew the vessel is now plunging in-system on a deliberate trajectory headed directly towards Earth.

Now the UNCC Nergal has a little over 90 hours to match course with the Fukunusubi, reconnoitre and attempt to prevent its terminal impact on the home world. Worse still, the first 80 or more of those hours will be spent in a stern chase to merely catch up before operations can begin. Once they enter the vessel, time will literally be of the essence; but it is not their *greatest* enemy. For onboard the derelict await hungering lifeforms whose alien biology pose an even greater danger...

Glossary

DCV: Deepspace Construction Vessel.

IED: Improvised Explosive Device.

IRV: Interstellar Research Vessel.

KBO: Kuiper Belt Object, a small planetoid orbiting out beyond Neptune.

ML-EM drive: Mach-Lorentz Electromagnetic Thrusters are reactionless engines which use microwaves to produce very low, but continual thrust that builds up over time.

RAM: Radar Absorbing Material.

STL: Slower than lightspeed.

UNCC: United Nations Customs Cutter.

UNSN: United Nations Solar Navy.

Player Briefing

You are the crew of the UNCC Nergal. A cutting edge, heavily armed military picket ship on its shakedown voyage. The ship has been set on an automated patrol of the outer reaches of the solar system somewhere near Neptune. Your primary task is to test all ship systems under rigorous conditions, whilst providing nominal peace-keeping and customs duties. Last you remember everything registered green when you went to sleep, seemingly only moments ago. Now, groggy and disorientated, you try to claw your way back to consciousness, alarms screeching in your ears. Something has gone wrong, but what? In fact what are you doing inside a glass coffin? Where on earth are you? Hell, what is your own name?

Chill Awakening

The characters start the game upon awakening from their hibernation pods, so-called Cold Sleep. Used to store a crew on tours of the outer system, UN picket ships are expected to remain on patrol for extended periods. Hibernation not only reduces life support requirements, but also slows subjective aging to 2.5% — or about 14 days on a normal two year tour, excluding those periods when the crew are awakened to conduct ship inspections or mount rescue operations.

Cold sleep technology is completely safe so, as a rule, crews suffer no repercussions when gradually emerging from hibernation. Unusually in this particular circumstance the UNCC Nergal's pods have brought the crew out of cold sleep using emergency flash-awakening procedures. Despite application of emergency stimulants, the characters experience the side effects of deep hypothermia, these being some difficulty speaking, sluggish thinking, and partial amnesia.

Due to the flash-awakening all skill checks performed by the characters during the first 72 hours suffer a penalty of Hard until their bodies fully recover.

To aid mutual recognition, each character has their name, rank and crew position printed in large block letters on the front of their hibernation flight suits. Games Masters may use this initial amnesia as the raison d'être to hand out the pre-generated characters (provided at the end of the scenario) to the players with no forewarning, and also encourage them to make name labels from folded paper.

The first thing the chilled characters notice after emerging from their pods is the alert warning flashing on every screen in sight. The message requires the captain to enter a voice and retina check before its contents are displayed, opposite.

A Gift From Shamash

FLASH OVERRIDE+++EMERGENCY ACTION MESSAGE+++TOP SECRET

Navy Tightbeam Message Y-EAM-736474

Sender: Admiral Suleiman, UN Navy Intelligence

Authorisation Code: Confirmed.

Recipient: Commander Romanov, UNCC Nergal

Message starts: Oort monitoring station Gamma Thirteen reports comm failure with DCV Fukunusubi. Vessel has failed to initiate deceleration manoeuvres. On ballistic course at 0.01c intersecting Earth projected 90 hours 11 minutes 23 seconds as of receipt of this message.

DCV Fukunusubi—Titan class deep space salvage and recovery ship. Last reported mission to recover Yu-anti extra-solar exploration asset. Vessel ceased communications 5 T-Days ago. Long range scans indicate slight rotation to vessel, suggestive of asteroid impact or explosive decompression.

You are ordered to intercept DCV Fukunusubi at flank speed. Investigate reasons for communication failure and prevent impact on homeworld – at all costs.

Message ends

> **Micrometeoroid Impact**
>
> *Travelling at low relativistic speeds poses great danger. Whilst cosmic and solar radiation are negligibly augmented at 0.01c, the energy of collisions with small physical objects increases catastrophically. If the Astrogation check is fumbled, the UNCC Nergal cuts through the ancient eccentric orbit of a small, long period comet. Passing through the near nebulous particle trail, the ship hits a scattering of sand grain sized particles which perforate the hull like a shotgun firing through cardboard.*
>
> *The resulting destruction should be determined randomly, however all the damage is light. Roll three times on the Ship Damage table (page 25) and describe the resulting catastrophe in terms likely to instil panic. Micrometeoroid Impact occurs at T-Minus 13 hours 49 minutes; leaving the crew only a few hours before intercept with the DCV Fukunusubi.*
>
> *A character may attempt an Engineering or Mechanics skill check [4 hours] to patch-up a single ship's system during that time. Multiple attempts on the same damaged area are not permitted, although a second character can augment the skill of the first if they also have the relevant skill.*

The scenario clock starts at T-Minus 90 hours, 12 minutes until predicted collision with Earth.

As the message implies, time is of the essence. Anyone with the Astrogation skill may attempt to plot a least-time intercept to match course and speed with the DCV Fukunusubi. Both the captain and pilot should possess the skill. Each Astrogation attempt costs the characters 10 minutes to program the flight computer and calculate the course. The results of the skill check are as follows:

- Fumble — Same as a success except the route passes through a cometary trail en route, causing the ship to suffer a micrometeoroid impact before interception—see boxed text above.

- Failure — Calculated course is too conservative, arriving after Earth impact. Try again.

- Success — Standard minimum distance course grants an intercept time of 83 hours.

- Critical — Using Neptune to slingshot reduces intercept time to 81 hours.

It is vital that the GM keep close track of passing time, or at least an illusion of it. If the characters do not manage to alter the trajectory of the Fukunusubi at least 90 minutes prior to collision, the vessel will have insufficient time to clear the planet and impact still occurs. Separating into task orientated teams is vital in order to succeed.

During the boarding and investigation of the Fukunusabi, using a skill to perform an action takes a finite amount of time (as indicated in brackets after the skill name). No time is used if the skill check is to come up with ideas or provide a hint.

Boarding

Regardless of whether the UNCC Nergal suffers a micrometeoroid strike en-route, the action really starts when the navy vessel intercepts the coasting DCV Fukunusubi. Orders state that the ship must be investigated to determine why communications have failed, in addition to diverting the vessel. There are several approaches the characters can take.

Analysing the Object

The Nergal possesses a sensor suite capable of providing extensive data on the drifting vessel. Interpreting the information requires a Sensors skill check:

- Fumble — The sensor operator triggers a catastrophic overload in the untested sensor system, inflicting Serious Damage (see Ship Damage table, page 25).

- Failure — Operator is only able to analyse half of the sensor data.

- Success — Operator correctly gathers the returned sensor data as described below.

- Critical—In addition to the data provided by a success, the operator locates an unsuited corpse floating 53km *outside* the Fukunusubi. This is the corpse of the captain, the only item of note being an old fashioned key on a chain about his neck.

The sensor suite provides the following information about the DCV Fukunusubi:

- RADAR: Vessel is experiencing a slow tumble about its longitudinal, lateral and vertical axes. Small amounts of debris currently orbit the unstable wreck in a roughly 5km radius.

- LIDAR: Vessel has a hull breach roughly 2m across in the mid section. No matching breach can be detected on the opposite side of the hull.

- Radio: Transponder still broadcasts ship's name, class and ID code, but at power conservation levels. No other communication can be established.

- Spectroscope: Vessel is surrounded by a very tenuous cloud of frozen oxygen, nitrogen and carbon dioxide, much of which has settled onto the hull.

- Radiation: No radiation detected, implying the fusion power plant is offline.

- Infrared: The majority of the ship has cooled to around -89 Celsius. Rear compartments are warmer, averaging approximately -41 Celsius.

- Visual: Dim pulsating red illumination, indicative of emergency lighting, still functions within crew areas possessing external portholes.

Scans confirm that the ship is indeed a Titan class salvage ship, used to travel to outlying installations in the Kuiper Belt, then either scrap or transfer them. At 195m long, 95m across the beam and massing some 23,000 metric tons, most of its bulk comprises of a massive work bay and two huge engines.

Taking the sensor readings at face value, it is unlikely that anybody is left alive. Whether or not the vessel is still functional cannot be answered from external scans.

Space Walking

Due to the Fukunusubi's tumble, direct docking with the Nergal or its shuttle is initially impossible. Boarding actions instead require an EVA approach (Extra Vehicular Activity). This means that some or all of the marines must first cross the intervening space in armoured vacc suits.

Such a boarding action is inherently hazardous. Whilst ambient radiation does not comprise any threat to the suited marines, attempts to physically land on the tumbling ship do. The best option is to land midway along the ship, near its centre of mass. All marines participating in the boarding action must roll against their EVA skill [15 minutes].

Radiation Threats During Spacewalks

At velocities of 0.01c energetic protons hitting space walkers at high speed (interstellar particles, coronal mass ejections and photons from solar flares) carry an energy of around 50KeV which are easily shielded against. Increasing speeds carry greater risks however. At speeds of 0.1c energy rises to 5MeV—the limit of radiation protection provided by marine vacc suits. Over this, particle radiation damage is lethal to anyone outside of a ship hull.

- **Fumble**—Marine fluffs the landing, suffering 1d6 damage to a random limb (ignoring suit armour) and rebounds into deep space. Worse still, their backpack manoeuvre system breaks requiring the shuttle to be prepped to rescue the floater [30 minutes].

- **Failure**—Marine impacts too hard causing 1d3 damage to a random limb (ignoring armour), but does not compromise suit integrity and maintains contact with the hull.

- **Success**—Marine lands safely without issue.

- **Critical**—Marine performs a spectacular space walk, arriving directly at the forward airlock.

After landing on the hull it takes the marines another 10 minutes to slowly make their way to the forward airlock where they can access the crew accommodation section. However, since the airlock lacks power, it must be manually cranked open, taking another 5 minutes of effort.

Attempting to enter the vessel via the hull breach would save the time clambering over the hull. Yet it is incredibly dangerous, requiring a second EVA skill check to bypass the razor sharp edges of what appears to be an internal explosion. Failing the roll results in the marine tearing their vacc suit, causing them to immediately start asphyxiating (see *Mythras Imperative* p28).

Patching a suit requires a successful Survival (Space) skill check. This suffers a penalty of Hard if performed on the marine's own suit, or Easy if patching another. If the first try fails, the self-adhesive patch is misapplied, failing to completely seal the rip. A second patch may be placed as per Reattempting Skills (*Mythras Imperative* p16), but if this also fails the tear cannot be sealed and the marine dies from decompression.

Stabilising the Tumble

Difficulties facing the marines don't stop after entering the DCV Fukunusubi. Until the tumble has been stabilised, all activities inside the vessel suffer a penalty of Hard due to the stomach-churning effects of the rotation, and any fumble rolled also includes the marine vomiting inside their helmet.

Normally the Titan class controls its orientation via gyroscopes, which obviously cannot be powered until the fusion plant is reignited. Fortunately for the boarding team, the ship possesses backup vernier thrusters powered by hydrazine. All they need to do is reach the bridge, then locate and trigger the emergency stabilisation system (ESS).

Once stabilised, the Nergal or its assault shuttle may freely dock with the main airlock, permitting any remaining marines and flight crew to board the Fukunusubi. Inside, there are signs of violence and madness everywhere. Games Masters are encouraged to stimulate the atmosphere of horror and paranoia. Most players at this point expect a bug hunt. Keep them guessing for a little while longer...

Exploration

Inside, the Fukunusubi is a nightmare mess. Corridors are dimly illuminated by pulsing red emergency lighting. Sealed areas are filled with slowly tumbling everyday objects. Assuming the characters requested an engineering layout of the Fukunusubi during their 80+ hour chase, provide them with rough ship deck plans. Otherwise the boarders need to find their own way around.

The salvage ship is a flattened oval shape with two huge drive sections mounted aft. Internally, it is designed as a series of decks stacked atop one another perpendicular to the direction of thrust. The bridge, crew quarters, stores, hibernation pods and manufactory are located in the tapered forward section. These are separated from the aft section by a vast repair bay with ventral doors. Engineering at the rear contains life support, the power plant and drive sections. Due to the low acceleration rates of ML-EM drives, its architecture is intended for near free fall use.

Two access tubes run the length of the of the ship. Portside is a lift shaft, starboard a ladder way. Both are designed to accommodate people wearing vacc suits. Deck access from these are via small, two-person internal airlocks, with reinforced outer bulkhead doors to provide extra structural strength.

Due to (as yet) unexplained events, the majority of the ship currently has no atmosphere. Assume a chamber is depressurised unless specifically stated in its description. Internal hatchways are sliding doors made of aerospace aluminium. Reinforced bulkhead doors located along the access tubes (and between the crew mess and bridge) are more massive, made of layered ceramic titanium, designed to resist extreme heat and radiation.

None of the currently closed doors can be opened until power is restored. Even then, some need to be overridden using the Electronics skill to bypass their security locks. Sliding internal hatchways can be burned-through using the thermite tape available in each marine's boarding kit, one roll per door (no skill check needed). Bulkhead doors cannot be burned-through in this manner, but require a breaching charge and a successful Demolitions skill check to blow-out the hinges.

Each deck of the ship is described in detail and takes 5 minutes to perform a quick search. Unless explicitly stated, initial discoveries are automatic, no Perception rolls needed. More detailed information may require application of specific skills or actions.

Bridge (Deck 1)

The bridge is accessible via a ladder in the ventral wall of the Crew Mess. Sealed off by an armoured bulkhead door, the only way to gain entry is either by restoring power and bypassing the security lock, or by blasting the door with breaching charges (as described previously).

Inside, the layout of the bridge is orientated vertically to the rest of the ship. It is cramped, with three massive flight chairs arranged in a triangular formation, surrounded by huge banks of avionics, sensors and system controls. Only a few lights remain blinking, but with the seat backs towards the boarders, nothing else can be seen save for the forward wall, which is a curved series of armoured crystal windows looking out into space.

Something small drifts out of the shadows into the faceplate of the first marine to enter the Bridge, extended teeth and claws reaching out towards his or her faceplate. This requires a successful Willpower roll or let out a yell of shock. If the character had previously stated that they had weapons prepared, a failure also causes the marine to let-loose a burst from their firearm, damaging some of the flight controls.

After any response has occurred it turns out that the object is a dead cat (a ginger tom), frozen in a rictus of fear. The only other thing of note in the compartment is the vacc suited figure of a dead crew member, still strapped into the pilot's chair. The captain and communication officers' seats are empty.

It requires a successful Perception skill check to locate the emergency stabilisation system [5 minutes], failure resulting in double the time taken. No further knowledge is required to activate the circuit, as it is completely automated and powered from its own backup battery. Merely pressing the interlocked buttons in sequence triggers the hydrazine thrusters, which then start to fire continuously, slowly countering the ship's tumble over a nauseating period of 10 minutes.

Two short passages lead from either side of the bridge. One leads to the ship's mainframe which is secured behind an electronically locked internal door. The other connects to the captain's cabin to which the door stands open.

The only thing of note in the captain's private quarters is a wall safe, inside which are the admin-level command codes for the mainframe, a set of well-worn orders (see *Salvaging Information* page 17) and a box of rounds for a 10mm pistol. The safe can only be opened using the key found around the captain's neck, i.e drifting 53km away. Lacking keys the safe can be blown open using the Demolitions skill [5 minutes], failure resulting in the con-

Deck Plans

UNCC NERGAL

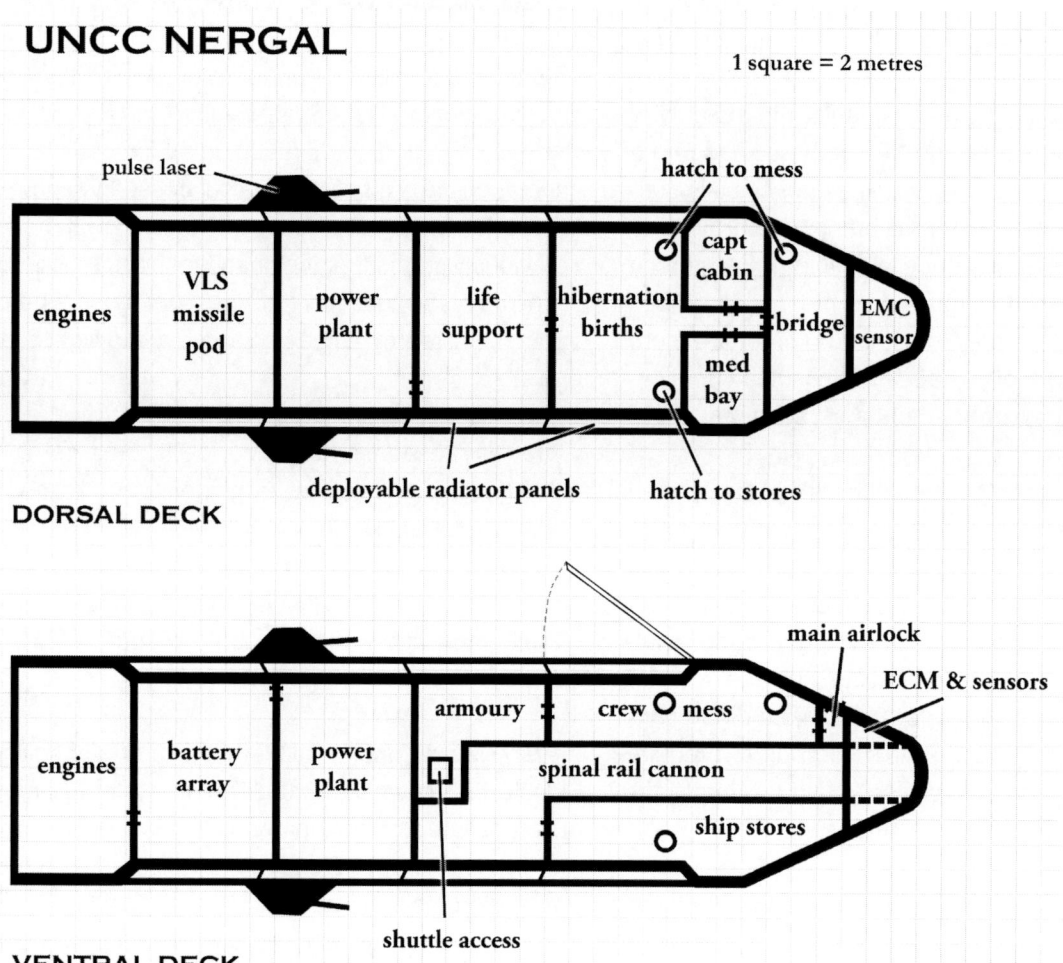

Size Comparison

A Gift From Shamash

DVC Fukunusubi

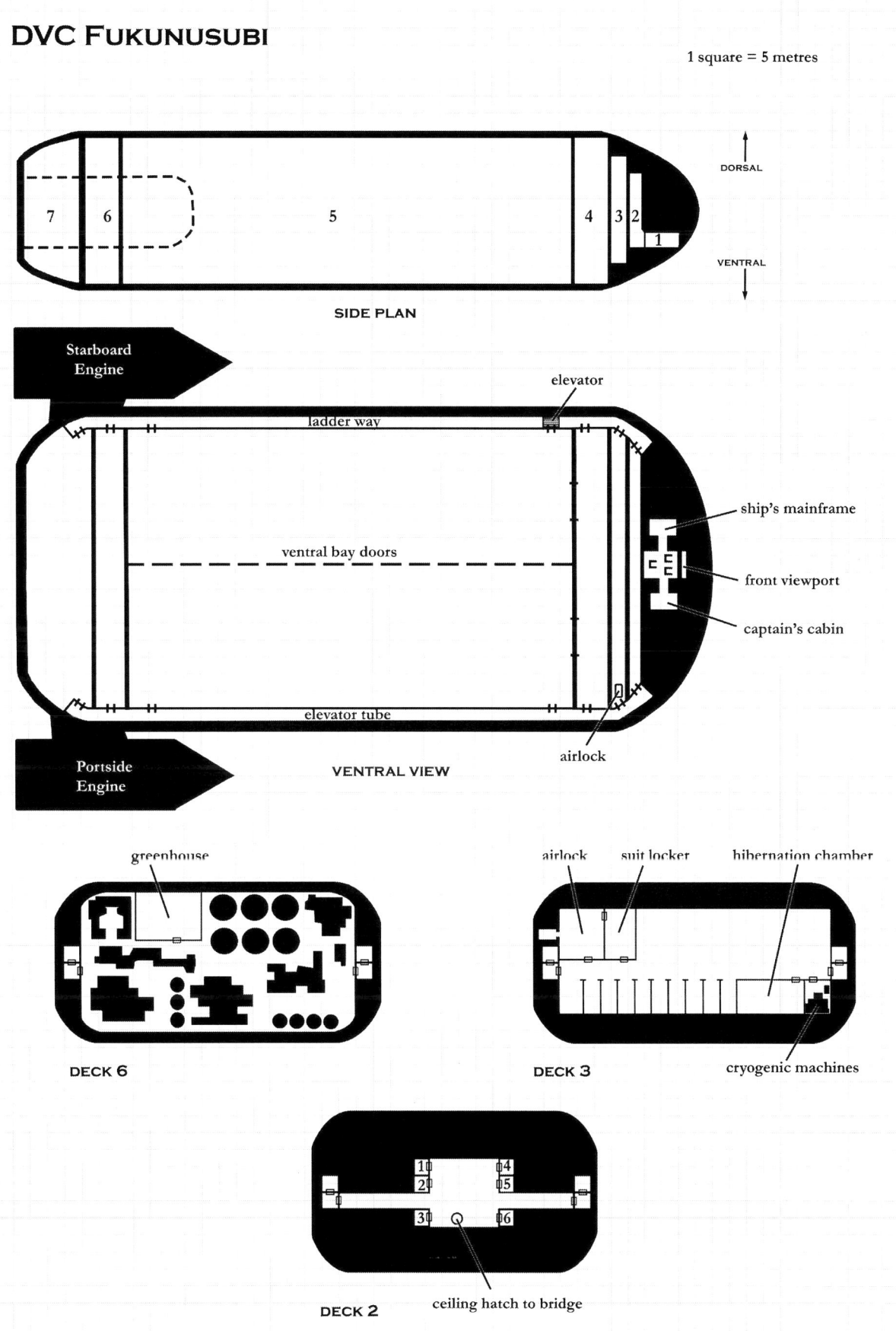

tents being destroyed and a fumble causing the ammo to touch-off (50% chance to hit someone in the cabin, causing 1d10 damage).

Ladder Access Tube (Decks 2-7)

This access tube has inset rungs leading most of the length of the ship, used only when the ship is operating under thrust. Its white walls are covered with contoured padding to prevent injury when floating along them.

A makeshift barrier of desks and mattresses are jammed into the shaft midway between decks 2 and 3, temporarily blocking access to the crew quarters and bridge. It takes 5 minutes to clear the obstacle. Half a dozen bullet holes riddle the padded walls leading back towards the manufactory bay, most likely pistol ordinance.

Lift Access Tube (Decks 2-7)

Similar to the ladder way, this tube extends most of the length of the ship. It is primarily intended for lifting supplies and other equipment between decks. Since it is an elevator shaft, the walls lack safety padding, instead possessing four inset runners for the lift's wheels.

The lift is positioned at deck 4, its doors open into the manufacturing bay. It remains inoperative even if power is restored, an Engineering or Mechanisms roll discovering that the cabin has been deliberately welded into its tracks. A small access panel opens in the roof of the cabin, but is too small to negotiate while wearing vacc suits.

Crew Mess (Deck 2)

An open area once used for meals and socialising, it is now full of floating plastic meal trays, cutlery and ruby droplets of frozen blood. The padded walls, ceiling and velcro floor are covered in black soot.

During investigation a blackened figure drifts out from behind the central table, one arm seeming to stretch towards one of the boarders. The gruesomely burned corpse appears to have blown-out its own brains. A second body, this one in a charred vacc suit, floats near the kitchenette, still armed with a shotgun. Its face is so contorted in terror that it is impossible to determine its sex, and there is no obvious cause of death.

Anyone checking the soot concludes it was the result of an internal fire, despite the fact that the ship is constructed from fire-retardant materials. After power is restored, a successful Electronics skill check [10 minutes] to hack into the ship's environmental controls reveals that decks 1 to 4 were deliberately vented, probably to prevent the spread of flames. Whilst a successful Science (Chemistry) or Demolitions skill check [instant] indicates that whatever started the fire was burning far hotter than simple oxygen.

Staterooms (Deck 2)

Six staterooms are adjacent to the crew mess. Each contains four sleeping cubicles (with their own entertainment screens) arranged two on either side, one above the other. Personal lockers are located at the end of the bunks, and a bathroom is located opposite the entry. All the plastic fittings are grimy from long use.

Doors to staterooms 2 and 5 are open, and have partially burned bodies in them. The remaining cabins are closed, but contain nothing interesting other than the personal effects of a rough, deep space salvage crew on extended deployments. (pictures of friends and loved ones, data chips of music and movies, spare jumpsuits, personal clothes, and sexy posters — both male and female).

Stateroom 2 contains a jumpsuit-wearing female. A successful First Aid skill check [instant] shows she was shot repeatedly in the face and body whilst lying medically restrained to her bed.

A Gift From Shamash

Stateroom 5 has a naked man floating in the bathroom. His eyeballs have been torn out (of which there are no sign). Strangely, there is plastic foam sprayed into the corners and edges of the bathroom.

Hibernation Chamber (Deck 3)

Used to transport the crew in cold sleep during cross-system transits, the room is filled with unmistakeable glass-fronted hibernation tubes. Although a backup system still maintains power, all but six of the 25 hibernation capsules have been wrecked. Something large and heavy was used to smash them. Five of the intact capsules contain a body dressed in undergarments, their stomachs massively distended, but none register any heart beat or respiration.

Locker Room (Deck 3)

Located adjacent to the main airlock, this is where the crew's vacc suits are stored. Thirteen heavy industrial suits are floating about the locker room and have what look like knife slashes through them. No blood, just cuts that render them non-functional.

Ship's Stores (Deck 3)

A two thirds empty compartment containing shelving that holds crates of freeze-dried food, beverages, spare jumpsuits, medicinal supplies, engineering spares and general emergency equipment. The weapons locker stands open, the only thing left within are three boxes of shotgun shells.

A successful Bureaucracy skill check [5 minutes] imparts that from a basic stock of three months, enough consumables remain to last an active crew for about two weeks. Rummaging through the engineering spares shows that many of the secondary and tertiary backup parts are missing. A successful Engineering roll suggests that this ship has been on an unusually long deployment.

Main Airlock (Deck 3)

The white padded airlock is empty save for a line of graffiti scrawled across the wall and floor. It reads *"May God have mercy on our souls"*. Nothing else of interest is here.

Manufactory Bay (Deck 4)

This deck is a mass of large scale industrial equipment, from plasma smelters to laser sintering printers. In skilled hands and enough time, the workshop can produce replacement parts for deep space installations or disabled ships. Until power is restored, this place is full of deep shadows and a multitude of hiding places.

Part of the forward bulkhead is warped upwards, its laminate structure badly cracked and melted. It looks like an explosion occurred, and there are some holes burned into nearby equipment. On one side of a larger piece of machinery (a microgravity ore grinder), is a thin smear of reddish material interspersed with white fragments, frozen in place. A successful Medicine skill check using a bio-analyser [5 minutes] disturbingly exposes the material as the remnants of a human head which was crushed into paste.

Repair Bay (Deck 5)

This gigantic bay encloses an internal space 130m long, 85m wide and 40m deep—big enough to swallow the UNCC Nergal with ease. Massive reinforced beams run the length of the bay along the dorsal, port and starboard hull. Despite its echoing volume, the bay is a scene of utter destruction.

Chains and cables wave gently in the vacuum. There is a ragged 2m diameter hole through the ventral doors, opening out into space, its edges discoloured and melted. Tool chests, scraps of unrecognisable metal, torn plastic, frozen organics, and a badly damaged industrial loader are drifting about, along with dozens of scintillating crystal shards (ranging from a few millimetres to a several centimetres in length) lodged in the walls and the heavy equipment bolted there.

These crystal shards appear to be parts of a shaped container, and close examination of a shard sets-off a marine vacc suit's radiation detection systems, warning of gamma ray emissions coming from the fragment. If somebody wishes to reconstruct the original shape, locating and scanning all the recoverable fragments takes several hours, risking a mild case of radiation poisoning in the process. The results of piecing the container back together are described on page 20.

Anyone with the Sensors skill can automatically analyse the shard emissions using a hand-held spectrometer (there is one in Stores on deck 3). The substance seems to be a form of synthetic sapphire, tinted with Radium-226 and Lanthium-137 on the inner surfaces, causing the crystal's soft radioluminescence.

Life Support (Deck 6)

Pressurised. If power has been restored before entry, the inner and outer airlock doors function correctly thereby avoiding any risk of explosive decompression (see *Power Plant*). The entirety of life support is filled with pipes, pumps, gauges, gas tanks and large vats of half-frozen biotic sludge. This is definitely the last place to engage in a firefight aboard the ship due to the risk of explosion or noxious chemical spills. There is a slight smell of chlorine in the air (if characters open their suits) which comes from what appears to be a corrosion leak in the side of a tank of sodium hypochlorite, over which a puddle of the chemical has formed. Inside are hidden several of the small alien creatures (page 21).

A small chamber on the dorsal side contains a greenhouse for growing fresh fruit and vegetables, whilst simultaneously augmenting carbon dioxide capture. The door into the greenhouse has been booby trapped, with a jury-rigged IED made of mining explosive. It looks like nothing more than a keypad crudely mounted above the hatch opening button. Any character with the Demolitions skill immediately recognises what it is. Otherwise, a successful Perception skill check is required to note that it looks out of place. If the hatch is opened before being deactivated, the display starts a countdown from five seconds. The GM should count down slowly. Players who state that their characters take cover before zero is reached are allowed an Evade roll to see if they dive clear in time. Those that fail, or make no effort to escape, are damaged by the mining charge. Roll 2d6 shrapnel damage against 3 separate Hit Locations. Any damage that overcomes the suit's Armour Points has breached its integrity, meaning it will depressurise the next time it is exposed to vacuum, unless repaired first (see Space Walking on page 7).

Inside the greenhouse are rows of withered plants, killed by the subzero temperature. A body also floats within trowel still in hand, their body a ruin of cruelly twisted limbs and a horrific facial expression, almost as if they had died in spasms of laughter. The only other thing of note is some sort of polythene tent set up over one of the potting beds, connected to several small gas cylinders (ammonia, carbon dioxide and methane).

The tent has been torn open, exposing a shrunken thing in a state of very advanced decomposition. Looking something like a head-sized coconut that has collapsed into itself, with oddly shaped tendrils that might be a rind or stalk. A sample can be taken for later study. Unknown to investigators is that the entire greenhouse is contaminated with alien spores, which aggressively infect investigators who enter with their helmets open, or later remove their vacc suits without first decontaminating them.

Power Plant (Deck 7)

Pressurised. The outer bulkhead hatch leading from the ladder access tube to the power plant section stands open, whilst the inner airlock door has been welded shut from inside the compartment. Cutting through with thermite tape results in explosive decompression, the blown out section striking anybody unprepared for such an eventuality (i.e. hasn't left the area or drilled a test hole through the door first) unless they succeed in a Formidable Evade skill check. Failure results in 3d6 damage to a single Hit Location as the sharp edged fragment ricochets around the airlock and lower access way. Any damage penetrating suit Armour Points causes suit decompression (see Space Walking, page 7).

After the door has been dealt with, investigation reveals that it has been damaged on the inside from a combination of irregular scratch marks and some sort of dark discoloration where the metal has corroded. A successful Science (Chemistry) skill check [15 minutes] recovers some biochemical residue, a form of fluorine-based acid whose molecular structure has disintegrated due to vacuum and temperature.

Inside, the majority of the deck is inaccessible due to the dense, complex machinery of the fusion plant. It is immediately apparent that parts of the reactor have been opened-up either to repair or sabotage it. Floating nearby is the body of the Fukunusubi's 1st officer. Blood has splattered the inside of his faceplate and his vacc suit has been torn open across the lower torso. Removing the body from the suit reveals a nasty abdominal wound.

Trying to restore power requires a character with the Engineering skill to reconnect everything [30 minutes]. The first attempt to restart the fusion plant automatically fails with an error message stating *<Foreign matter blocking ignition>*. Further investigation discovers a second body, that of the chief engineer, hidden inside the ignition chamber where he bottled himself up and eventually suffocated, ruptured eyes bulging, and tears still frozen on his cheeks.

Hidden deep within the other machines is one of the larger alien creatures (page 23), which slowly awakens over the course of several hours before it begins hunting.

Moving the Fukunusubi

To prevent the Fukunusubi from colliding with Earth, the characters must either bring the ship's engines back online, or somehow destroy the vessel and hope the fragments don't survive atmospheric re-entry. A task which will might be made harder if individual characters are attacked by the alien lifeforms aboard the ship.

Ideas to connect the Nergal and Fukunusubi together, by welding or using cables, will not work. The navy cutter is covered by a thick RAM layer and lacks tow points which would compromise its stealth capabilities. Simply pushing the vessel off course will not work either, as the acceleration produced by the Nergal's ML-EM engines is insufficient to move the 23kT vessel far enough off course in the few hours remaining.

Repairing the salvage ship requires jump starting the derelict's fusion reactor to provide power for the drives, then rebooting the computer to access the navigation controls. With the emergency batteries drained to critical levels, the characters need to be creative and succeed in the following skills—some of which can be worked on concurrently:

- *Jump starting the fusion generator: Engineering skill [2 hours], requires scavenging a 500m long high voltage power line from the repair bay to connect both ships' power plants*

- *Booting up the ship's mainframe: Computers skill [30 minutes], requires Admin password locked in the Captain's safe, tight-beaming Earth for the manufacturer reset code [1d3+3 x 10 minutes], or hacking the operating system—a Formidable Computers roll [15 minutes]*

- *Repairing avionics and navigation: Electronics skill [45 minutes], assuming the controls have not been damaged*

- *Calculating a new course vector: Astrogation skill [10 minutes], the previously locked-in course deliberately targets Osaka (more specifically the Yuanti corporate headquarters located there).*

- *Initiating course change: Pilot skill [1 minute]*

The alternate plan of destroying the Fukunusubi is technically beyond the ability of the UNCC Nergal, whose weapons are more designed for incapacitating ships, rather than annihilating them. The only destructive method that would work actually needs the characters to not stabilise the Fukunusubi's tumble, but instead use the following plan:

- Cannibalise six missile warheads: Mechanics skill [2 hours]

- Attach warheads to the reinforced structural beams in the repair bay: Demolitions skill [30 minutes]

- Jury-rig the emergency stabilisation system to only fire one set of the ventral thrusters, thereby increasing its spin: Electronics skill [15 minutes]

- Blow the warheads so that the ship flies apart in two halves, at the exact moment they are perpendicular to its vector: Astrogation skill [5 minutes]

If completed correctly, the wreckage will pass either side of Earth. Any failures during the first two steps results in the ship failing to separate, thus continuing on to its original target and obliterating most of central Japan. Failing only one or both of the last two steps ends up with half of the Fukunusubi striking Earth off the coast of Southend-on-Sea (in the UK), wiping out Kent and Essex in a 50Mt airburst.

Salvaging Information

With the entire crew dead or missing it is obvious why no communications could be established with the Fukunusubi. What caused the psychopathic killing spree is less obvious, and answers will be demanded from Navy Intelligence.

By now the characters should be spooked, especially if one or two of them have been killed during the brief bursts of microwave static (see The Extraterrestrial Lifeform page 21). There are multiple sources of information they can gather:

- Personal Records from the Ship's Logs
- Navigational Data from the Black Box
- Environmental Settings in Life Support
- Performing Autopsies on the Crew
- Analysing the Decomposed Plant
- Piecing together the Crystal Fragments
- Reading the Captain's Orders
- Requesting Information from UNSN

Personal Records

All the sensor feeds and data pads aboard ship are merely dumb terminals that access the Fukunusubi's mainframe. Recovering information from its databanks therefore requires that power be restored before it can be rebooted.

Characters in a rush may propose simply yanking its solid state memory drives and taking then back to the Nergal, which is easily done, no skill check necessary. However, subsequently trying to read the seriously outdated devices without its accompanying hardware, first requires a roll against the Electronics skill [30 minutes] to create an interface cable, followed by a Computers skill check [75 minutes] to knock together an emulator for the drive's archaic protocol. Failure simply means the tasks take double the time to complete.

Once running, it quickly becomes obvious that the drives holding mission data have been deliberately purged. Running a low level data recovery program recovers a few fragmentary bits of information for analysis.

Navigational Data

The data drive containing recorded navigational data has not only been scrubbed, it also has two 10mm bullet holes punched through it. If the characters think of it, the ship's black box should have a copy of all its movements. Embedded in the bulkhead between decks 2 & 3, it is accessible with some difficulty and can be removed by succeeding in a Mechanics skill check [45 minutes].

Examining the black box shows that the ship has travelled a very circuitous route using slingshot manoeuvres about several major Kuiper Belt objects. To calculate where it intercepted its target and where the Fukunusubi dragged it to, requires a successful Astrogation skill check at Formidable difficulty [15 minutes]. What the characters do with this information depends on how the scenario progresses, and may force whoever is left in command to make an ethical choice.

Environmental Settings

Anyone searching for the reason why several decks were depressurised might think to check the state of the ship's environmental settings. This can be done in either of two places. The first is the manual control panel in Life Support (requiring a successful Engineering skill check to interpret). The second is via the environmental bridge terminal if power is restored.

Recoverable Mission Data Fragments

Most of the recoverable mission data is tiny scraps of text written in the ship personnel logs. A couple are several seconds-long segments of video, captured during some sort of salvage operation. No time stamps remain, but they are presented in sequential order as recorded into the memory drive. It is suggested that the Games Master give them out piecemeal as each new fragment is recovered.

Text—"ried about how far we are travelling into the Oort region, crew mollified by the prospect of triple pay though they remain unaware of the true nature of our mis"

Text—"re grumbling from the comms lockdown after accepting this recovery mission. Performed the fifth course change since we started. The chief gave us all a bollocking last shift for starting a sweepstake on our target's origins, which only caused the scuttlebutt to incre"

Text—"s I reported previously, even the Fukunusubi's drives will take weeks to decelerate the vessel so I recommend we return to cold sleep until its relocated. Enough salvage here to make us all wealthy beyond our dreams, especially considering its nature. Captain is being very tight lipped about where we are supposed to stash the literal antiqu"

Video Sequence—2.79 second B&W suit camera feed taken inside what appears to be a spaceship, although fittings seem at least a century out of date. Vessel is obviously a derelict, ice crystals cover every surface, glimmering in the suit lights. Harsh breathing can be heard followed by the start of a curse as the camera pans over a skeleton dressed in an unfamiliar jumpsuit. (Freezing the frame and studying the suit patch returns the word Shamash)

Video Sequence—3.34 second B&W clip taken in what appears to be a massive cargo hold. The view zooms in to what appears to be a standard trunk-sized container, its lid partially ajar from which plant-like stalks emerge, their tips spread in five-lobed flowers. As the camera closes in, the clip frizzles out in a burst of static, as audible radiation warnings start chiming in the background.

Text—"hink I've been working too long. Tired, headaches, itching eyes. I suppose I'd better check with the engineer that atmospherics haven't cocked up again. Need a showe"

Text—"mand we covertly return to the labs on Triton. So many deaths, and they knew. Those bastards knew about SIRb013e. I'm no longer trusted. Panic and paranoia has spread. I have to stop this before its too lat"

The manual controls in Life Support show that decks 1-4 have been deliberately vented. The safety interlocks overridden. A series of warning lights for internal fire, contaminated atmosphere, air filter blockage and decompression are still dimly lit.

Using the bridge terminal reveals a sequence of triggered alerts. Time settings are scrambled, but a partial log exists in its buffer. Strangely, they start with a contamination warning on deck 5 (excessive chlorites), then a particle clogging alert in air filtration in Life Support. After this are several cross references to medical alerts triggered on deck 5, followed by deck 2. Next is a warning that fluoride levels are critically low, followed by another contamination warning on deck 6 (deadly levels of chlorites), an explosive decompression on deck 4, and then a fire on deck 2. Last entry in the log notes the bypassing of atmosphere safety interlocks, after which decks 1-4 were deliberately evacuated.

A Gift From Shamash

Personnel Autopsies

Thirteen bodies remain aboard the Fukunusubi, plus the captain's body floating 53km away from the ship. Due to time constraints and lack of a crew member fully trained in post-mortem techniques, any autopsy will be superficial and must be performed on the Nergal which has a small operating room.

Discovering the following information requires a successful Medicine skill check [15 minutes] for each corpse:

Captain's body floating 53km away: Died from rapid decompression, which should be patently obvious since he wasn't wearing a suit. No signs of violence.

Seated body on bridge: Died from slow asphyxiation when her suit's life support expired. Face still bears an expression of grim determination.

Burned body in Crew Mess: Brains blown out contiguous to being burned. Exposed areas (face and hands) are burned down to the bone. Bullet holes in skull match calibre of pistol held in left hand.

Suited body in Crew Mess: Died from massive cardiac arrest. Vacc suit prevented burning.

Body in Stateroom 2: Died from bullet wounds prior to burning. Has severe abrasion damage on wrists and ankles where she was restrained.

Body in Stateroom 5: Died from brain embolism. There are fragments of his own fingernails in the eye sockets.

5 bodies in Hibernation Pods: All appear to have died from chronic pulmonary edema and show some degree of fibrosis (scarring) in the lungs. Blood toxicology reports fatal levels of hydrogen fluoride and oxygen difluorides. Swollen stomachs are a natural by-product of decomposition in an aerobic environment; i.e. they are filled with gas from slow rotting.

Body in Life Support: Death from seizure, likely caused by massive amounts of swelling in the brain, sinuses and eyes. Blood toxicology shows traces similar to those in the Hibernation Pods.

Eviscerated body in Power Plant: Died from something cutting into his stomach. Victim also suffered lacerations to the oesophagus and throat, almost as if something passed upwards and exited the mouth. Swabs taken from the injury will, if chemically tested, reveal traces of non-human biological material.

Body hidden in fusion generator: Although initial evidence suggests suffocation, the victim actually mirrors symptoms exhibited by the body in Life Support. Namely a massively swollen brain, sinuses and eyes, the latter of which show signs of massive cancerous growth.

Important Note—the bodies from Life Support and inside the Fusion Generator both contain second-stage organisms which were hibernating due to the falling temperature levels on the Fukunusubi. As they warm-up, the creatures begin to recover, meaning that the character examining the bodies will likely encounter the creatures. The Games Master must decide how many recuperate, and whether they use the opportunity to escape into the rest of the Nergal using their active camouflage, or attack the person performing the autopsy.

Analysing the Plant

Not much survives of the strange plant discovered in the greenhouse. A DNA test is only possible on board the Nergal to characters with the Science (Biology) skill [1 hour]. Success reveals that the 'organic material' is clearly non-terrestrial in origin. However it is impossible to discern if it has been artificially created as part of illegal bio-research; or if it originated from some other star system.

Whoever performs the analysis is exposed to the alien spores. See *The Extraterrestrial Lifeform*.

Reassembling the Crystal Fragments

Reassembling a virtual model using the scans taken from the shards requires a successful Computing skill check [45 minutes] run on the Nergal's mainframe. The result is three partial images, the best 90% complete, of objects closely resembling canopic jars a metre tall, 50cm at the widest point, topped with an unrecognisably-shaped lid and a vertical line of strange sigils down one side.

Reading the Captain's Orders

A single sheet of well-worn plastic, these orders have obviously been read and reread countless times. The printout displays the contents of a self-erasing comm-mail sent from the headquarters of the Yuanti Corporation some three years previously. The text of the massage reads:

"Self Purging Mail 1562783. Attention Captain DCV Fukunusubi. Message begins: You are hereby ordered to abandon smelter reclamation mission and divert to 90482 Orcus, whereupon you shall stock your vessel with as much provisions, water and fuel as you can conveniently stow. If questioned about your destination, you will state that you have been directed to perform a resupply mission to Com-Am mining base 1138. Instead, under strict radio silence, you will take your vessel on as indirect course as possible, avoiding other shipping and installations and unnecessary emissions, to intercept Yuanti sample return asset at V774104. You shall then take asset under tow, relocating it at pre-determined KBO of your choice. Upon arrival you will conceal asset, thereafter perform preliminary investigation. Unless you shall be of an opinion that your salvage crew cannot handle what they find, take aboard significant discoveries and return to Yuanti research centre on Psamatha, taking all care to conceal route. To prevent risk of mutinous discontent, all crew are granted triple pay as compensation for extended hardship, plus bonuses on receipt of whatever is found. All company policies concerning corporate secrets and presumptive early cessation of contracts apply, as per exec order 90125."

Requesting Information from UNSN

Characters may wish to send questions to the UNSN to help them with certain elements of their investigation, such as the manufacturer reset code for the derelict's mainframe computer. Despite being in control of policing the solar system, the UNSN has only limited authority to demand information from the most powerful megacorps. Thus many questions will prove unanswerable and establishing a direct link with anyone of consequence at the Yuanti Corporation proves impossible.

Frequent requests for information results in the UNSN ordering comms silence for security reasons. However, three key questions the UNSN can answer are:

Who and what is the Yuanti Corporation?

The Yuanti Corporation—Est. 21st C. Created as one of many companies in direct competition to Musk Industries, Yuanti specialised in bioengineering and were the first to patent gene replacement therapies to help adapt humanity to extended micro gravity. Profits from their breakthrough helped the corporation branch into aerospace technology, asteroid mining and robotics. During the exploration diasporas of the early-mid 22nd Century, Yuanti borrowed heavily against projected future profits to build and outfit six interstellar missions, all of which either discovered nothing of interest or failed to report back and were considered lost with all hands. The financial repercussions resulted in Yuanti having to sell two major KBO planetoids and its shipbuilding and robotic subsidiaries. It is now regarded as a second tier corporation primarily focussed on biosphere engineering, with secondary concerns salvaging old mining installations and the manufacture of infantry-level armaments.

Have Yuanti exhibited any strange activity of late?

Nothing of note for several years. If anything, Yuanti has been exhibiting a scrupulous accordance with solar system law and has allowed free access to its weapon facilities for UN inspection—which is unusual behaviour for a megacorp. Prior to that it was suspected that Yuanti had been the target of corporate sabotage, when three and a half years ago their main deep space communications relay on 42355 Typhon shut down completely and remained offline for 41 days.

Where was the DCV Fukunusubi last reported?

Last reported docking of the DCV Fukunusubi was thirty seven months ago at the Veylandi Resupply Station on 90482 Orcus. Stated course logged with Kuiper Belt traffic control was to Com-Am mining base 1138. The vessel failed to dock with the facility however, engaging in a slingshot manoeuvre deeper into the belt, destination unknown. No further contact was knowingly made as the DCV Fukunusubi deactivated its transponder during flyby. An outstanding fine still stands for contravention of the Law of System Space, 33CFR 401.20.

What was the Shamash and what was its purpose?

The IRV Shamash was one of six sister ships, the Aten, Helios, Istanu, Koyash, Shamash and Thesan built by Yuanti Corp for the exploration of nearby stars for habitable planets, new mineral resources and the collection of astrophysical data. The missions were ruinously expensive; not only from developing interstellar capable vessels, but also in the stipend paid to the UN to purchase ownership of any discoveries made at each star. The Aten , Istanu and Koyash returned with data which proved to be universally disappointing. What faint traces of life were found, were little more than bacteria, whilst metals and minerals found were no different from their terrestrial counterpoints. The Thesan was destroyed en-route to its star, whilst the Helios suffered a fatal failure of its fusion plant, leaving the crew to die a slow death that resulted in a PR disaster. Nothing was ever heard from the Shamash (launched towards Sirius in 2107) though the ship did send an arrived safely message. Only other item of note lies in the personnel selected for the Sirius mission, most of whom were recruited ex-military and a few of the planetary science team appear to have been cross trained in areas such as anthropology or archaeology.

THE LIFEFORM

The primary threats to the crew of the Nergal are the somnolent alien creatures infesting the derelict. Exposed to heat they slowly awaken and begin to hunt for food. After several weeks at severe sub-zero temperatures the remaining lifeforms are very hungry indeed.

SIRb013e is a dual-phase life cycle organism which starts out as an immobile plant that flowers, and then violently disperses a fine pollen if contact is made with the bloom. Any spores landing on the ocular organs of a higher order animal infest the eye, overwriting its DNA structure and converting it into the organism's second stage form, a sort of worm with pentaradial symmetry, the optic nerve splitting into five hook-tipped tentacles.

Infection to conversion takes between 4 and 7 days. The host creature initially suffers visual hallucinations leading to increasing psychosis as frontal lobe brain tissue is subsumed. The parasite repurposes the tissue, granting itself limited sapience. Terminal phase is extremely rapid, involving blindness shortly followed by extreme agony, then death when the creature tears itself free through the victim's ocular orbit.

After the partially developed second stage leaves its host, its primary concern is locating sources of kerogens (from which it produces protective waxes to contain its own halogen-based metabolism) and gorges itself, growing rapidly until its bulbous end reaches a diameter of almost half a metre. Lacking its primary form of nutrition the organism consumes long chain hydrocarbons, polypropylene plastics or the body fat of other animals instead.

Once it achieves full growth, it is driven to find a place to bury itself and enters a torpid state. Its waxy skin thickens, metamorphosing into a type of tough cellulose designed to protect it against hos-

> **The Best Horrors Are Unseen**
>
> *These nasty creatures are the main enemy of the adventure. Game Masters are encouraged to keep the players unaware of their existence for as long as possible, but tantalise the characters with occasional sounds or imagined movements in peripheral vision to raise tension. The actually number of aliens is up to the Games Master to decide, depending upon whether they want the majority of the characters to survive or not.*
>
> *When they do come out to play, at a suitably tense moment, the Games Master should stage an attack on a lone character, or duo if the players are being paranoid. If Perception rolls fail to spot their subtle polychromatic camouflage then victim(s) should not be permitted to know what is attacking them.*
>
> *As the first attacks will be from behind, the first few ambushes are likely to result in fatalities; particularly since communications during each attack will be overwhelmed by microwave static and nobody will be able to call for help. This is intended, being part of the psychological ratchet turning of the adventure. If the group dislikes character death, a few NPC marines can be the first ones killed and partially eaten.*
>
> *Once they wise-up to the situation, the Games Master can decide how to end the scenario. Either picking off crew members off one by one, sending a wave of small beasts to swamp them if they fortify themselves in one location, or letting them escape the Fukunusubi only to discover an individual has sneaked aboard hidden on the back of a suit.*

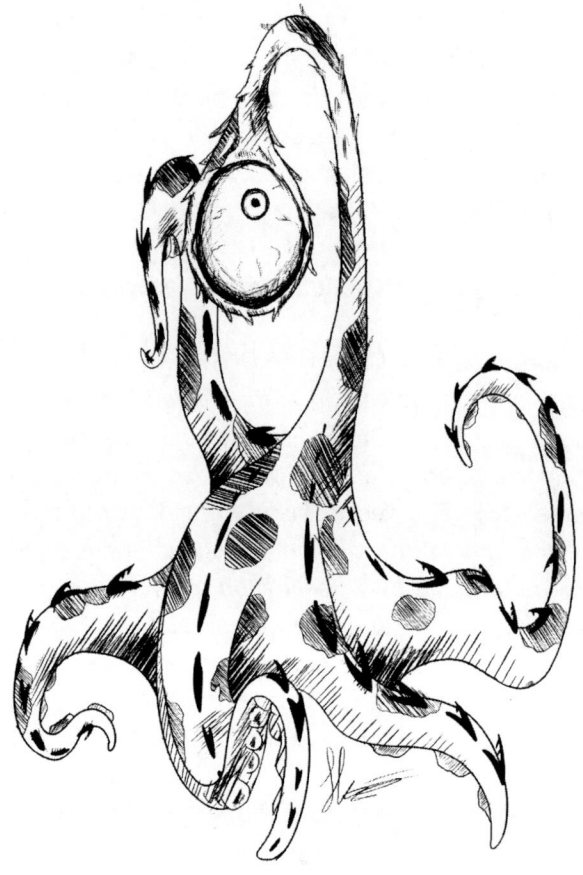

tile environments. Internally, the stolen brain tissue and musculature slowly liquefy into a nutrient-rich soup.

Torpor can last decades. Only when the now fully plant-like gourd detects a combination of movement and warmth (anything above -37°C) does it grow a new stalk, which flowers into a five lobed bloom—dark purple in the visible spectrum, but scintillating in UV light—ready to start the cycle again.

Ostensibly the SIRb013e organism appears to have evolved to cope with extreme or unstable seasonality. Its home world probably spends much of its orbital period at severe subzero temperatures, whilst the atmosphere is likely low in free oxygen and water, yet rich in halogens. Its secondary form can survive low pressures, and even vacuum, for several hours.

Body chemistry is based upon chlorine trifluoride, which is violently corrosive against organics, glass and most metals such as tungsten and titanium. If punctured, its body fluids will ignite human skin on contact. Above 11°C these fluids boil, forming a colourless gas which causes respiration failure at low concentrations of several hundred parts per million, or simply destroys the lungs at higher densities, as ClF3 reacts violently with water to produce hydrofluoric and hydrochloric acid.

2nd Stage	Attributes
STR: 1d3+3 (5)	Action Points: 2
CON: 1d3+5 (5)	Damage Modifier: -1d6
SIZ: 1 (1)	Movement: 6 metres
DEX: 2d6+3 (10)	Initiative Bonus: +12
INS: 2d6+6 (13)	Armour: None
POW: 1d6 (4)	Abilities: Camouflaged, Gnaw, Incendiary, Shrieker

Skills: Athletics 55%, Brawn 26%, Endurance 40%, Evade 60%, Perception 47%, Stealth 73%, Track 58%, Willpower 38%

1d20	Location	AP/HP
01-10	Eyeball Body	0/3
11-12	1st Tentacle	0/1
13-14	2nd Tentacle	0/1
15-16	3rd Tentacle	0/1
17-18	4th Tentacle	0/1
19-20	5th Tentacle	0/1

Combat Style: Alien Swarm (Tentacles, Bite) 45%

Weapon	Size/Force	Reach	Damage	AP/HP
Tentacles	S	S	Grip Effect	0/1
Burrowing	S	S	1d4	0/3

3rd Stage	Attributes
STR: 1d6+9 (13)	Action Points: 2
CON: 1d6+6 (10)	Damage Modifier: -1d2
SIZ: 3 (3)	Movement: 8 metres
DEX: 2d6+3 (10)	Initiative Bonus: +12
INS: 2d6+6 (13)	Armour: Thorny Skin
POW: 2d6 (7)	Abilities: Camouflaged, Gnaw, Incendiary, Shrieker

Skills: Athletics 63%, Brawn 56%, Endurance 60%, Evade 70%, Perception 50%, Stealth 73%, Track 63%, Willpower 44%

1d20	Location	AP/HP
01-10	Eyeball Body	3/4
11-12	1st Tentacle	1/2
13-14	2nd Tentacle	1/2
15-16	3rd Tentacle	1/2
17-18	4th Tentacle	1/2
19-20	5th Tentacle	1/2

Combat Style: Alien Hunter (Tentacles, Bite) 63%

Weapon	Size/Force	Reach	Damage	AP/HP
Tentacles	M	M	Grip Effect	1/2
Burrowing	S	M	1d6	3/4

SIRb013e 2nd Stage (eye sized)

Small specimens of its secondary form cooperate to swarm larger prey, using their chromatophoric skin to camouflage themselves and lay ambush. The first attack uses their tentacles to grip onto the Hit Location struck, after which they hold on and begin to burrow into the victim's body (the eyeball segmenting open into a threefold set of jaws). The organism uses the Sunder special effect if its prey possesses a carapace or armour.

SIRb013e 3rd Stage (football sized)

Larger specimens are tougher and more confident about taking on prey singlehandedly, still relying on stealth to gain surprise. It applies complex strategies to isolate a lone victim, fleeing if threatened. Afterwards it evolves its tactics, using traps or tools to enhance its next assault.

Creature Abilities

Camouflaged: Organism is adept at hiding due to its colouration or unusual surface texture. Those attempting to spot the creature suffer a penalty to Perception of two difficulty grades; or only one difficulty grade if using the IR sensors mounted on Marine vacc suits. When not hiding, the creatures send warnings by using their polychromatic skins to broadcast hypnotically pulsating patterns.

Gnaw: The creature is adept at chewing itself into the body of a victim it has gripped using its tentacles. This allows the creature to spend an Action Point on its Turn to automatically roll damage without needing an attack roll, whilst also permitting it to ignore any negative Damage Modifier it might normally possess. Rolled damage is first applied to any protection worn, permanently reducing its Armour Points until they reach zero, then continuing against the flesh underneath. The victim cannot parry or evade the attack - only try to pull it free on their turn.

Incendiary: If the organism is damaged its greenish-yellow blood immediately bursts into flame igniting an Intensity 3 Fire (Mythras Imperative p29) on whatever it was touching, which lasts for three rounds even in non-oxygen atmospheres. Although the creature itself does not catch fire, it will be consumed by the released heat unless it can scuttle clear. The blood chemistry is so highly oxidising it burns through any substance in a corrosive manner (eating away Armour Points), even explode on contact with water. If the blood emerges in temperatures above 11.75°C it boils, reacting with moisture in the air to create acid—which causes a further 1d3 acidic damage to everything within a 3m range. Vacuum or rapid decompression disperses the incendiary blood, preventing any damage after the first round.

Shrieker: Creature sends out paralysing bursts of electromagnetic radiation in the MHz to GHz wavelengths when it attacks a victim. Unfortunately for lifeform SIRb013e, this has no effect on humans, but it does disrupt their suit microwave comms, flooding the airwaves with disturbing static screeches. Anyone ambushed by the creatures is cut off electronically, both audio and visual, until the alien or their victim is dead.

What Next?

Assuming any of the characters survive (and that the players do not run screaming from this psychotic adventure), the Games Master has the option of continuing the investigation of the mystery. They have several options available to them.

They could return to Neptune and assault the Yuanti research centre on Psamatha. Obviously the station is engaged in some form of illicit studies, perhaps alien-based bio-weapons. Such actions might provoke a war between the UNSN and certain corporations, but if Yuanti is allowed to get away with smuggling alien life forms, who knows what might happen when, ultimately, one gets loose. In fact, what will happen if none of the characters realises that one of their own crew might currently be infected?

Alternatively the Nergal could try to locate the wreck of the *IRV Shamash*, hidden somewhere in the outer Kuiper Belt. What other secrets could the ship contain, recovered from the Sirius System? Its cargo bay is loaded not only with plant and animal specimens, but also archaeological fragments of an alien civilisation. Of course after the Fukunusubi screw-up, Yuanti will be scrambling to send their own security team to recover the vessel before the UNSN decides to destroy it.

Either route eventually leads to a wealth of hitherto bogus alien conspiracy theories, which seem to have been researched extensively by corporate xenologists. The scientists postulated that alien intelligence was linked to Sirius (Alpha Canis Majoris), based their research on a number of stories from ancient mythology.

The first hints came from Babylonian tales of Annedoti 'the Repulsive Ones' who came from the sky in a great egg and lived in the sea. Sumerian myths portrayed Ea (or Enki) the god of wisdom who lived in 'Apsu', a submarine palace; and Oannes, the amphibian diety who taught them mathematics, astronomy, agriculture and writing. Brief mentions continued throughout the classical period of wise, amphibian deities. In these myths the star Sirius was sometimes refered to.

Most archaeologists would have let the matter rest as an example of the spread of cultural polytheism. However, during 1946 a remote tribe named the Dogon was discovered, and they displayed astounding astronomical knowledge. Their priests knew that Sirius was a binary star system, and also that the lesser star, Sirius B, was coloured white, and had an elliptical orbit that lasted 50 years. Since Sirius B was never proven to exist until 1970, when the first photograph was taken of it, the source of this information staggered the French anthropologists Griaule and Dieterlen.

After this revelation, the crew of the Nergal might be prompted into travelling to Sirius themselves. Enough supplies remain aboard the Shamash to restock, if they are willing to take the chance. But if organism SIRb013e is anything to go by, they are going to face an extremely hostile world...

Ship Damage

Every time a spaceship suffers damage that penetrates its hull, there is a chance that a vital subsystem has been affected. Depending on which system has been hit, the effects of subsystem damage can be catastrophic. Fortunately, micrometeoroid impacts cause only light damage.

The damage a starship can suffer is similar to that of characters. Light Damage can be repaired in hours, Serious Damage in days and Major Damage needs a dockyard to rebuild the destroyed subsystem. Subsystems that are damaged but not yet destroyed, suffer a loss in functionality as represented on the table below. Repeated harm to the same subsystem does not increase the detrimental effect unless the damage level increments.

Ship Damage Table

1d10	System	Light Damage Result	Serious Damage Result	Major Damage
1	Avionics	Pilot rolls suffer a difficulty grade of Hard	Pilot rolls suffer a difficulty grade of Formidable	Ship can no longer be steered or change course
2	Communications	Comms rolls suffer a difficulty grade of Hard	Comms rolls suffer a difficulty grade of Formidable	Ship can no longer communicate or spoof enemy sensors
3	Crew	1d3x10% of off-duty crew (and passengers) suffer a Major Wound and must succeed in an Endurance roll or be killed instantly	1d6x10% of off-duty crew (and passengers) suffer a Major Wound and must succeed in an Endurance roll or be killed instantly	Everyone aboard the ship dies in catastrophic atmospheric and life support failure
4	Engines	Ship acceleration is reduced by 1d3x10%	Ship acceleration is reduced by 1d6x10%	Ship can no longer change its velocity
5	Fusion Reactor	One powered subsystem is taken off line due to power loss.	An additional 1d3 powered subsystems go off line	Ship is destroyed in a cataclysmic explosion
6	Hibernation Pods	1d3x10% of the pods suffer power surges precipitating their occupants back to wakefulness	1d6x10% of the pods are heavily damaged inflicting a Major Wound on their occupants	Entire hibernation section is destroyed along with anyone still in them
7	Life Support	Crew suffers a universal penalty of Hard to all skills due to bad air and loss of heat	As Light Damage but the situation becomes critical, raising the penalty to Formidable	Entire crew is killed due to the release of poisonous gases unless they enter suits
8	Sensors	Sensors rolls suffer a difficulty grade of Hard	Sensors rolls suffer a difficulty grade of Formidable	Ship is rendered blind
9	Shuttle Bay	Shuttle cannot launch or dock	Shuttle takes damage and becomes inoperable until repaired	Shuttle and everything else in the bay is destroyed
10	Weapons (Roll if more than 1)	Weapon's damage is halved	Weapon is rendered inoperable	Weapon explodes inflicting its normal rolled damage to another subsystem within the ship

UNSN Characters

This adventure comes with a set of experienced pre-generated characters for ease of play. However, some Games Masters may wish to let their players create their own characters, with an eye towards running their own campaigns using this scenario as a launching point.

If players wish to make their own characters, they should follow the steps described in Mythras Imperative on pages 4-10 (or use the *Mythras* full rules, *M-Space*, or even *Luther Arkwright*). Since the adventure is military science-fiction, replace the Culture and Careers available to the characters with those described below, noting the Military Occupational Specialities option.

Culture: UN Citizen

All characters are citizens of the United Nations. Although the UN does not hold political authority over the outlying colonies, humanity has become socially and educationally homogenised. Wealth and rank disparities still exist, as does corporate repression on certain planetoids. However there are ostensibly universal rules concerning employment rights, criminal punishment and vocational training. Everyone speaks English as their native tongue, but may learn an archaic national language as one of their Professional Skills if desired. Note that everyone in the UN lives in peaceful communities protected (or perhaps enforced) by specially trained security forces. Therefore characters do not have access to a cultural Combat Style.

Standard Skills: Deceit, Drive, Influence, Insight, Locale, Perception, Willpower.

Professional Skills: Bureaucracy, Commerce, Craft (any), Courtesy, Language (any), Science (any), Streetwise.

Careers: UNSN Military

Under UN mandate, a citizen who joins the military is subject to a severe restriction in personal freedom, in return for focussed training. In game terms this means that characters use the 100 points designated for career skills for Basic Training, then apply the additional 150 points normally assigned for rounding out to their Military Occupational Speciality instead. Generous Games Masters may increase the number of points as desired.

For the purposes of this adventure, characters have two military paths available: Navy or Marines.

Marine Basic Training

Marines are the troops assigned to naval vessels and installations. The predominant focus is on close combat and survival.

Standard Skills: Athletics, Customs (Marines), Endurance, Evade, Unarmed, Willpower; Combat Style (Firearms)

Professional Skills: EVA, Gambling, Lore (Squad Tactics), Navigation, Streetwise, Survival (Planetary), Survival (Space).

Navy Basic Training

Navy personnel are assigned to the flight, maintenance and weaponry of spaceships, orbital defence platforms, dockyards and the like. Their training is biased towards technical skills.

Standard Skills: Brawn, Customs (Navy), Dance, Endurance, First Aid, Unarmed, Willpower.

Professional Skills: Craft (any), EVA, Gambling, Mechanics, Science (any), Streetwise, Survival (Space).

Military Occupational Specialties

After basic training, a character in the UNSN can choose a military occupational speciality (MOS). Unless specifically stated, some specialities are available to both navy and marine characters. For example the Pilot speciality can be taken by either marines or navy ratings. No matter which speciality taken, UNSN marines are expected to pick-up a rifle and fight with their squad when called upon.

Each MOS lists a number of skills and combat styles, any of which can be learned. Additionally characters may also assign their points into those standard skills available during basic training. *For instance a marine who decides to train as a Medic could, if desired, also allocate some of their skill points into Evade and Unarmed (standard skills for Marine basic training).*

UN Marine Combat Styles:

Firearms: Any shotgun, grenade launcher or rifle; Micro-G Combat & Ranged Marksman traits

Sidearms: Any pistol; Micro-G Combat trait

Blades: Any knife or dagger; Micro-G Combat and Throw Weapons traits

Heavy Weaponry: Heavy squad support and vehicle mounted weapons; Spray and Pray trait

Gunnery: Any ship or shuttle mounted weapon; Predictive Targeting trait

UN Navy Combat Styles:

Sidearms: Any pistol; Micro-G Combat trait

Scrapper: Any knife, dagger or engineering tool; Hidden Weapons trait

Gunnery: Any ship or shuttle mounted weapon; Predictive Targeting trait

Assault Troop (Marines)

Assault troops are best described as career grunts. As combat specialists they train in a range of combat styles as well as honing their general skills, such as Endurance, Evade and Unarmed.

MOS Skills: Comms, Demolitions, Drive, EVA, Sensors; Combat Style (Blades), Combat Style (Heavy Weaponry).

> **New Trait Descriptions.**
> *Micro-G Combat*—allows the user to ignore the skill cap placed upon combat rolls by the EVA skill, using techniques such as firing from their centre of mass, bracing against a solid object, or holding onto their opponent.
>
> *Predictive Targeting*—permits the user to ignore the skill cap placed upon ship-to-ship combat rolls by the Pilot skill of the helmsman, assuming his own vessel is jinking.
>
> *Spray and Pray*—grants the user to automatically apply the Pin Down special effect against targeted foes (in addition to any others they gain), provided they fire on full automatic.

Engineer (Navy)

Engineers are responsible for maintaining and repair of mechanical systems aboard a spaceship. They look after the drives, power plants, life support and numerous other subsystems.

MOS Skills: Computers, Craft (any), Engineering, Electronics, Mechanics, Perception; Combat Style (Scrapper).

Gunner

Gunners are either navy or marine personnel, trained in the operation of ship weapons such as lasers or torpedo tubes. They often possess diverse skills in order to service their particular weapons.

MOS Skills: Craft (any), Electronics, EVA, Mechanics, Perception, Sensors; Combat Style (Gunnery).

Medic/Doctor

Marine medics are trained to give emergency medical treatment in the field, whereas navy doctors serve as full physicians.

MOS Skills: First Aid, Insight, Medicine, Research, Science (Primary Speciality), Science (Secondary

Speciality), Willpower. Select science specialities from Biology, Chemistry, Pharmacy, Psychology or Xenology.

NCO/Officer

This speciality covers the skills required to command others. It is usually reserved for marines or navy personnel who exhibit a level of technical competence and nascent leadership skills. For the purposes of character generation, assume that this speciality grants the officer an extra set of skills in addition to their original MOS. Officers, according to their rank, also gain a bonus number of points which can only be spent on whichever command skills are selected: marine corporal (leads a fireteam) + 50 points; marine sergeant (leads a section) +100 points; navy warrant officer (leads a ship section) +50 points; navy midshipman +25 points; navy lieutenant +50 points; navy commander +100 points.

MOS Skills: Bureaucracy, Courtesy, Influence, Lore (Squad Tactics) or Lore (Ship Tactics), Oratory, Teach, Willpower; Combat Style (Sidearms).

Operations (Navy)

Operations specialists, also known as deck officers, supervise the key systems necessary to steer a spaceship safely on its voyage. They have a number of subspecialties based upon the equipment they monitor. Navigation, sensors, comms, conning, tactical and so on. Although the position is known as a deck officer, within the UNSN it is a courtesy rank only, since on smaller ships the role is usually taken by common ratings.

MOS Skills: Astrogation, Comms, Computers, Electronics, Lore (Ship Tactics), Pilot, Sensors.

Pilot

Pilots are trained to fly interplanetary and aerospace craft to carry out a wide variety of tasks. Navy pilots learn to control full size spaceships during space warfare, whilst marine pilots focus more on small fighter craft and assault shuttles.

MOS Skills: Astrogation, Comms, Lore (Ship Tactics), Navigation, Pilot, Sensors; Combat Style (Gunnery).

Recon (Marines)

Marine reconnaissance specialists are tasked with providing their commander with information about the operational area. Missions focus on stealthy insertion to observe and report, as well as lay ambushes or provide a tactical distraction.

MOS Skills: Demolition, Navigation, Perception, Stealth, Survival (Planetary), Track; Combat Style (Blades).

Technician (Marines)

A combination of armourers, data slicers, snipers and a number of other sub-specialties, a technician fulfils the role of maintaining a marine unit's weapons, armour and vehicles. They additionally provide mission-critical skills such as methods of bypassing security systems, hacking computers or opening locked doors.

MOS Skills: Computers, Craft (any), Electronics, Lockpicking, Mechanics, Perception, Sensors.

EQUIPMENT

Navy Vacc Suit—4 Armour Points (-6 Initiative Penalty), 6 hours life support, comms, 1 use patch repair kit.

Marine Vacc Suit—8 Armour Points (-6 Initiative Penalty), 12 hours life support, local-range comm link, tactical HUD (map projection, squad member location displays), IR sensors, range finder, 2-use suit patch repair kit, 4 equipment pockets located on Chest (2) and Legs (2) each one capable of holding 2 spare clips, one roll of thermite tape, or a breaching charge.

AK-774 Assault Carbine—Hypervelocity flechette firing gauss rifle, rated for vacuum use. The low penetrator dart ammunition is designed to flatten against rigid surfaces limiting damage to vital ship systems, thus rounds only cause 2d6 damage.

Remington 1066 Automatic Shotgun—Boarding weapon intended to clear corridors of lightly armed foes using cartridges filled with soft plastic capsules. These deform on impact to temporally incapacitate victims (shooter can choose the Stun Location special effect, but cannot use Impale). Shots scatter causing 1d8 Damage to 1d3 contiguous Hit Locations at short range, or 1d6 Damage to 1d4 adjacent Hit Locations at medium range.

H&K 7mm Pistol—See Pistol (*Mythras Imperative* p27)

Combat Knife—See Dagger (*Mythras Imperative* p27)

Thermite Tape—Can burn through one internal door per roll. Vulnerable to unprompted ignition if in close proximity to a sufficiently hot fire (see Incendiary ability of the alien lifeform), in which case it inflicts 1d6+6 damage to the Hit Location it is carried in.

Breaching Charge—Can blow through one bulkhead hatch per charge. Comes with remote detonator that links with suit comms.

Medical Scanner—Able to perform an internal scan of physical injuries, with additional functionality to analyse blood and other biological samples.

Technician Kit—A complete gadget set for electrical engineering, computer slicing and an omnitool for simple mechanics. Fits snugly into a Marine vacc suit equipment pocket.

Engineer's Tools—A trunk-sized toolbox incorporating everything from socket wrenches to a portable arc welder. Weighs 50kg.

NERGAL CREW MEMBERS

The following characters have been pre-generated for the convenience of Games Masters who wish to run the adventure without the complication of character generation. There are fifteen experienced characters to choose from, six naval and nine marines, granting most groups plenty of backups if the death toll is high.

Flight Crew

The flight crew manage the ship during patrols; setting its course, observing sensors and coordinating manoeuvres during intercepts of possibly hostile craft. Most of the systems are heavily automated, requiring little oversight or maintenance during the crew's long stretches in Cold Sleep.

Commander Romanov—Captain and tactical officer.

Lieutenant Petrie—Comms and sensor operator.

Chief Petty Officer Macintosh—Power and drives engineer.

Able Rate Clarkson—Navigator and pilot.

Able Rate Toranaga—Electronics, computer and weapons technician.

Medical Officer Brahmaja—Surgeon and customs inspector.

Marines

The marines provide a dual role aboard the Nergal. First and foremost they are the boarding team sent to inspect vessels for customs violations. However, they also double up as gunnery officers and damage control teams if and when the ship is engaged in battle. Outside of combat it is the marines who perform the supernumerary tasks of cleaning, mess duties, mechanical servicing and anything else their sergeant can think of to keep them out of trouble.

Charlie Team

Sergeant Jurgenson—Assault Specialist

Lance Corporal Spatts—Assault Specialist

Marine Jones—Technician Specialist

Marine Vladimir—Gunnery Specialist

Delta Team

Corporal Schlarger—Recon Specialist

Marine Moreau—Assault Specialist

Marine Mumba—Assault Specialist

Marine Biwa—Corpsman

Shuttle Pilot

Corporal Hawker—Marine Shuttle Pilot.

> ### Character Action Points
> *Mythras Imperative assigns 2 Action Points to every character. In the full Mythras rules, Action Points are variable. We have given the variable number of Action Points for each character in parantheses in the Attributes section of the stat block.*

A Gift From Shamash

Commander Romanov

One of the original interstellar starship captains, Romanov is a wealthy man from extended coldsleep bonuses, he has sickened of Earth and its megacorps, being a man 'out of his time'. Haunted by the stark beauty of deep space he joined the UNSN to isolate himself from frivolous humanity, but still be at the controls of a starship.

Romanov	Attributes
STR: 10	Action Points: 2
CON: 15	Damage Modifier: None
SIZ: 15	Movement: 6 metres
DEX: 7	Initiative Bonus: +12
INT: 17	Armour: None
POW: 12	
CHA: 17	

Standard Skills
Athletics 49%, Brawn 59%, Conceal 38%, Customs 47%, Dance 57%, Deceit 39%, Drive 51%, Endurance 53%, Evade 35%, First Aid 34%, Influence 84%, Insight 78%, Locale 40%, Perception 37%, Stealth 44%, Unarmed 73%, Willpower 84%

Professional Skills
Astrogation 93%, Bureaucracy 62%, Comms 63%, Courtesy 51%, Craft (Scrimshaw) 58%, EVA 65%, Gambling 39%, Lore (Ship Tactics) 84%, Mechanics 46%, Navigation 50%, Oratory 68%, Pilot 57%, Science (Astrophysics) 55%, Sensors 62%, Streetwise 43%, Survival (Space) 62%, Teach 49%

Passions
Dislike Corporate Culture 74%, Loyalty to UNSN 81%, Recount Nostalgic Memories 66%

1d20	Location	AP/HP
01–03	Right Leg	0/6
04–16	Left Leg	0/6
07–09	Abdomen	0/7
10–12	Chest	0/8
13–15	Right Arm	0/5
16–18	Left Arm	0/5
19–20	Head	0/6

Combat Style: Combat Style (Sidearms) 59%

Weapon	Size/Force	Damage	Notes
Antique Pistol	H	1d8	Jams after first shot if fired in vacuum

Lieutenant Petrie

An ex-belter, Petrie was badly injured in a suspicious claim-jumping incident. Six months of reconstructive surgery later, he followed the advice of his corporate lawyer to drop the case, accepting a moderate payout and volunteered for the navy. Petrie was soon placed on picket ship duty posted to the outer regions of the solar system, where he continues to work on an advanced thesis concerning the lack of alien civilisations detected.

Petrie	Attributes
STR: 12	Action Points: 2
CON: 9	Damage Modifier: None
SIZ: 10	Movement: 6 metres
DEX: 9	Initiative Bonus: +12
INT: 15	Armour: None
POW: 15	
CHA: 12	

Standard Skills
Athletics 29%, Brawn 35%, Conceal 54%, Customs 63%, Dance 38%, Deceit 50%, Drive 43%, Endurance 43%, Evade 47%, First Aid 35%, Influence 71%, Insight 54%, Locale 62%, Perception 55%, Stealth 39%, Unarmed 61%, Willpower 69%

Professional Skills
Astrogation 58%, Bureaucracy 56%, Comms 81%, Courtesy 56%, Craft (Lapistry) 67%, EVA 77%, Gambling 35%, Lore (Ship Tactics) 61%, Mechanics 52%, Oratory 55%, Pilot 60%, Research 79%, Science (Geology) 71%, Sensors 85%, Streetwise 36%, Survival (Space) 80%.

Passions
Inquisitive 70%, Find Evidence of Intelligent Life 64%, Loyalty to UNSN 54%

1d20	Location	AP/HP
01–03	Right Leg	0/4
04–16	Left Leg	0/4
07–09	Abdomen	0/5
10–12	Chest	0/6
13–15	Right Arm	0/3
16–18	Left Arm	0/3
19–20	Head	0/4

Combat Style: Combat Style (Sidearms) 63%

Weapon	Size/Force	Damage	Notes
H&K 7mm Pistol	L	1d6	Low power ammunition for shipboard use

Able Rating Clarkson

Young, overconfident navy hand who showed himself to be an excellent ship's pilot and weapons officer. Enlisted in the navy as soon as he could leave Earth. His brother, a marine, was killed in a boarding action against asteroid miners turned pirate. He looks to the captain as a source of inspiration, but watches far too many action movies to be healthy.

Clarkson	Attributes
STR: 9	Action Points: 2 (3)
CON: 12	Damage Modifier: None
SIZ: 12	Movement: 6 metres
DEX: 17	Initiative Bonus: +16
INT: 14	Armour: None
POW: 10	
CHA: 12	

Standard Skills
Athletics 51%, Brawn 47%, Conceal 49%, Customs 62%, Dance 48%, Deceit 58%, Drive 83%, Endurance 50%, Evade 54%, First Aid 46%, Influence 40%, Insight 38%, Locale 52%, Perception 51%, Stealth 49%, Unarmed 59%, Willpower 45%

Professional Skills
Astrogation 67%, Comms 45%, EVA 81%, Gambling 55%, Mechanics 37%, Navigation 48%, Pilot (Starships) 92%, Sensors 62%, Streetwise 59%, Survival (Space) 53%

Passions
Arrogant 60%, Hate Pirates & Hijackers 64%, Loyalty to UNSN 42%

1d20	Location	AP/HP
01–03	Right Leg	0/5
04–16	Left Leg	0/5
07–09	Abdomen	0/6
10–12	Chest	0/7
13–15	Right Arm	0/4
16–18	Left Arm	0/4
19–20	Head	0/5

Combat Style: (Scrapper) 63%

Weapon	Size/Force	Damage	AP/HP
Switchblade	S	1d4	6/6

Chief Petty Officer Macintosh

A genius in mechanics and engineering the chief maintains the drives and power systems, whilst also repairing secondary based equipment on board the Nergal. Traditionally grumpy and always complaining at the manoeuvres which Clarkson (the pilot) sometimes puts 'his' ship through. In reality he has a acerbic wit and genuine love of both the ship and its crew.

Macintosh	Attributes
STR: 14	Action Points: 2
CON: 16	Damage Modifier: +1d4
SIZ: 17	Movement: 6 metres
DEX: 9	Initiative Bonus: +12
INT: 14	Armour: None
POW: 12	
CHA: 15	

Standard Skills
Athletics 39%, Brawn 55%, Conceal 46%, Customs 61%, Dance 56%, Deceit 47%, Drive 56%, Endurance 60%, Evade 41%, First Aid 46%, Influence 71%, Insight 55%, Locale 54%, Perception 56%, Stealth 42%, Unarmed 79%, Willpower 57%

Professional Skills
Computers 38%, Craft (Machinist) 60%, Engineering 83%, Electronics 72%, EVA 48%, Gambling 60%, Mechanics 77%, Science (Physics) 66%, Streetwise 51%, Survival (Space) 59%

Passions
Rage and Curse 81%, Hate Dirt & Grime 64%, Loyalty to the Nergal 60%

1d20	Location	AP/HP
01–03	Right Leg	0/7
04–16	Left Leg	0/7
07–09	Abdomen	0/8
10–12	Chest	0/9
13–15	Right Arm	0/6
16–18	Left Arm	0/6
19–20	Head	0/7

Combat Style: (Scrapper) 65%

Weapon	Size/Force	Damage	AP/HP
Wrench	M	1d6+1d4	6/10

Able Rating Toranaga

Utilises most electronic equipment to the max. His specialities lie in sensors, communications, computers and cryptography. Being an expert in code breaking, he has a tendency to snoop in people's email boxes, or read their personal logs.

Toranaga	Attributes
STR: 7	Action Points: 2
CON: 14	Damage Modifier: None
SIZ: 14	Movement: 6 metres
DEX: 5	Initiative Bonus: +12
INT: 18	Armour: None
POW: 10	
CHA: 9	

Standard Skills
Athletics 44%, Brawn 41%, Conceal 58%, Customs 41%, Dance 56%, Deceit 41%, Drive 61%, Endurance 38%, Evade 45%, First Aid 40%, Influence 47%, Insight 39%, Locale 54%, Perception 39%, Stealth 55%, Unarmed 35%, Willpower 52%

Professional Skills
Comms 70%, Computers 77%, Craft (Electrical Circuits) 74%, Electronics 80%, EVA 40%, Gambling 43%, Mechanics 58%, Science (Cryptography) 59%, Sensors 82%, Streetwise 38%, Survival (Space) 37%

Passions
Despise non-military 76%, Gregarious 55%, Loyalty to UNSN 53%

1d20	Location	AP/HP
01–03	Right Leg	0/6
04–16	Left Leg	0/6
07–09	Abdomen	0/7
10–12	Chest	0/8
13–15	Right Arm	0/5
16–18	Left Arm	0/5
19–20	Head	0/6

Combat Style: (Scrapper) 59%

Weapon	Size/Force	Damage	AP/HP
Coffee Mug	S	1d4	3/4

Medical Officer Brahmaja

The ship's doctor is bored most of the time. Brahmaja ran off to join navy when some eugenics experiments inspired by the work of a historic German doctor backfired and created some horrific mutant births. He started taking stimulants to focus on his work, but is now hopelessly addicted.

Brahmaja	Attributes
STR: 13	Action Points: 2 (3)
CON: 12	Damage Modifier: +1d4
SIZ: 12	Movement: 6 metres
DEX: 12	Initiative Bonus: +14
INT: 16	Armour: None
POW: 13	
CHA: 11	

Standard Skills
Athletics 49%, Brawn 44%, Conceal 61%, Customs 52%, Dance 45%, Deceit 77%, Drive 64%, Endurance 45%, Evade 41%, First Aid 86%, Influence 36%, Insight 61%, Locale 36%, Perception 59%, Stealth 47%, Unarmed 42%, Willpower 41%

Professional Skills
Craft (Narcotics) 58%, EVA 38%, Medicine 77%, Research 87%, Science (Biology) 80%, Science (Chemistry) 80%, Science (Xenology) 68%, Streetwise 60%, Survival (Space) 43%

Passions
Addicted to Stimulants 74%, Guilt Complex 76%, Pacifist 56%

1d20	Location	AP/HP
01–03	Right Leg	0/5
04–16	Left Leg	0/5
07–09	Abdomen	0/6
10–12	Chest	0/7
13–15	Right Arm	0/4
16–18	Left Arm	0/4
19–20	Head	0/5

Combat Style: None—tries to surrender or flee combat

Sergeant Jurgenson

A hard core sergeant in charge of the entire marine section, Jurgenson leads Charlie fire team during boarding actions. Middle aged, foul mouthed, but warm hearted he is loved by the men, as he watches their backs in combat and takes the place of a surrogate father if they need to talk. Has more combat missions to his name than the rest of the squad put together.

Jurgenson	Attributes
STR: 11	Action Points: 2 (3)
CON: 17	Damage Modifier: +1d2
SIZ: 15	Movement: 6 metres
DEX: 11	Initiative Bonus: +13 (+7 in Armour)
INT: 14	Armour: Marine Vacc Suit
POW: 11	
CHA: 17	

Standard Skills
Athletics 55%, Brawn 50%, Conceal 46%, Customs 57%, Deceit 44%, Drive 55%, Endurance 79%, Evade 70%, First Aid 46%, Influence 77%, Insight 82%, Locale 49%, Perception 60%, Stealth 59%, Unarmed 80%, Willpower 75%

Professional Skills
Bureaucracy 35%, Comms 44%, Demolitions 33%, EVA 83%, Lore (Squad Tactics) 84%, Navigation 63%, Oratory 57%, Streetwise 56%, Survival (Planetary) 51%, Survival (Space) 84%, Teach 55%

Passions
Swear Vociferously 80%, Hate Incompetence 59%, Loyalty to UNSN 95%

1d20	Location	AP/HP
01–03	Right Leg	8/7
04–16	Left Leg	8/7
07–09	Abdomen	8/8
10–12	Chest	8/9
13–15	Right Arm	8/6
16–18	Left Arm	8/6
19–20	Head	8/7

Combat Style: Blades 76%, Firearms 88%, Heavy Weapons 69%

Weapon	Size/Force	Damage	AP/HP
Combat Knife	S	1d4+1+1d2	6/8
AK-774	H	2d6	Vacc Rated Assault Rifle

Corporal Hawker (Pilot)

Hawker is the archetypal gung-ho marine pilot. Cocky, full of himself and willing to do anything for a bet; however he is still very well trained. As a pilot he receives a courtesy rank, yet remains outside the fire team chain of command since he is responsible for shuttling other grunts around. Any jarhead who pisses him off can expect to suffer a vomit inducing ride the next time they are assigned boarding duty.

Hawker	Attributes
STR: 14	Action Points: 2 (3)
CON: 13	Damage Modifier: None
SIZ: 11	Movement: 6 metres
DEX: 14	Initiative Bonus: +15 (+9 in Armour)
INT: 15	Armour: Marine Vacc Suit
POW: 8	
CHA: 11	

Standard Skills
Athletics 61%, Brawn 56%, Conceal 44%, Customs 56%, Deceit 64%, Drive 53%, Endurance 65%, Evade 62%, First Aid 48%, Influence 45%, Insight 42%, Locale 63%, Perception 60%, Stealth 46%, Unarmed 64%, Willpower 50%

Professional Skills
Astrogation 66%, Comms 50%, EVA 86%, Gambling 61%, Lore (Ship Tactics) 64%, Lore (Squad Tactics) 43%, Navigation 37%, Pilot (Shuttles) 77%, Sensors 65%, Streetwise 41%, Survival (Planetary) 52%, Survival (Space) 54%

Passions
Seat-of-the-Pants Flying 77%, Gambling 69%, Loyalty to UNSN 48%

1d20	Location	AP/HP
01–03	Right Leg	8/5
04–16	Left Leg	8/5
07–09	Abdomen	8/6
10–12	Chest	8/7
13–15	Right Arm	8/4
16–18	Left Arm	8/4
19–20	Head	8/5

Combat Style: Firearms 59%, Gunnery 81%

Weapon	Size/Force	Damage	AP/HP
AK-774	H	2d6	Vacc Rated Assault Rifle

Corporal Schlarger (Recon)

Cool, level headed and thoughtful, Schlarger makes careful plans before sending Delta fire team into action. She hates 'gung-ho' personalities, and will slap down any marine who mentions the words 'bug hunt'! Well respected by her men since she likes to lead by example and is not afraid to join combat.

Schlarger	Attributes
STR: 12	Action Points: 2 (3)
CON: 15	Damage Modifier: None
SIZ: 13	Movement: 6 metres
DEX: 13	Initiative Bonus: +14 (+8 in Armour)
INT: 13	Armour: Marine Vacc Suit
POW: 15	
CHA: 15	

Standard Skills
Athletics 64%, Brawn 41%, Conceal 58%, Customs 58%, Dance 34%, Deceit 32%, Drive 55%, Endurance 71%, Evade 88%, First Aid 40%, Influence 57%, Insight 63%, Locale 74%, Perception 81%, Stealth 79%, Unarmed 77%, Willpower 65%

Professional Skills
Bureaucracy 42%, Courtesy 34%, Demolition 44%, EVA 68%, Lore (Squad Tactics) 77%, Navigation 82%, Oratory 60%, Streetwise 55%, Survival (Planetary) 78%, Survival (Space) 81%, Teach 46%, Track 69%

Passions
Do Everything by the Book 70%, Ruthlessly Honest 56%, Loyalty to UNSN 81%

1d20	Location	AP/HP
01–03	Right Leg	8/6
04–16	Left Leg	8/6
07–09	Abdomen	8/7
10–12	Chest	8/8
13–15	Right Arm	8/5
16–18	Left Arm	8/5
19–20	Head	8/6

Combat Style: Blades 50%, Firearms 73%, Heavy Weapons 70%

Weapon	Size/Force	Damage	AP/HP
Combat Knife	S	1d4+1	6/8
AK-774	H	2d6	Vacc Rated Assault Rifle

Lance Corporal Spatts (Assault)

Reserve Delta fire team leader, Spatts is intelligent but over full of testosterone. He deeply respects sergeant Jurgenson, always trying to pre-emptively prepare Delta team for commands he assumes the sergeant will issue (often getting it wrong). His behaviour covers an inherent fear of failure, perhaps leading to the loss of one of his team.

Spatts	Attributes
STR: 14	Action Points: 3
CON: 11	Damage Modifier: +1d2
SIZ: 16	Movement: 6 metres
DEX: 16	Initiative Bonus: +14 (+8 in Armour)
INT: 12	Armour: Marine Vacc Suit
POW: 7	
CHA: 12	

Standard Skills
Athletics 57%, Boating 40%, Brawn 60%, Conceal 41%, Customs 49%, Dance 37%, Deceit 45%, Drive 57%, Endurance 67%, Evade 77%, First Aid 39%, Influence 53%, Insight 45%, Locale 39%, Perception 58%, Ride 46%, Sing 41%, Stealth 59%, Swim 43%, Unarmed 74%, Willpower 50%

Professional Skills:
Comms 54%, Demolitions 55%, EVA 80%, Gambling 56%, Lore (Squad Tactics) 63%, Navigation 49%, Sensors 52%, Streetwise 52%, Survival (Planetary) 58%, Survival (Space) 64%

Passions
Always Second Guess the Sergeant 70%, Fear of Failure 81%, Loyalty to UNSN 52%

1d20	Location	AP/HP
01–03	Right Leg	8/6
04–16	Left Leg	8/6
07–09	Abdomen	8/7
10–12	Chest	8/8
13–15	Right Arm	8/5
16–18	Left Arm	8/5
19–20	Head	8/6

Combat Style: Blades 50%, Firearms 73%, Heavy Weapons 70%

Weapon	Size/Force	Damage	AP/HP
Combat Knife	S	1d4+1+1d2	6/8
AK-774	H	2d6	Vacc Rated Assault Rifle

Marine Biwa (Corpsman)

The marine section's medic, Biwa possesses a grim sense of humour. He has lost enough marines on his watch to understand the lethal nature of close combat in space, to the point where his comrades now call him Dr Death. In his spare time he tattoos the crew with whatever art, mottos or decorations they wish.

Biwa	Attributes
STR: 12	Action Points: 2 (3)
CON: 15	Damage Modifier: None
SIZ: 13	Movement: 6 metres
DEX: 13	Initiative Bonus: +16 (+10 in Armour)
INT: 13	Armour: Marine Vacc Suit
POW: 15	
CHA: 15	

Standard Skills
Athletics 52%, Brawn 59%, Conceal 38%, Customs 44%, Dance 50%, Deceit 39%, Drive 36%, Endurance 55%, Evade 69%, First Aid 88%, Influence 36%, Insight 63%, Locale 39%, Perception 59%, Stealth 55%, Unarmed 57%, Willpower 64%

Professional Skills: Craft (Tattooist) 79%, EVA 75%, Lore (Squad Tactics) 37%, Medicine 78%, Navigation 47%, Research 53%, Science (Pharmacy) 76%, Science (Psychology) 83%, Streetwise 41%, Survival (Planetary) 49%, Survival (Space) 68%

Passions
Crack Inappropriate Joke 87%, Fatalistic 69%, Loyalty to UNSN 50%

1d20	Location	AP/HP
01–03	Right Leg	8/5
04–16	Left Leg	8/5
07–09	Abdomen	8/6
10–12	Chest	8/7
13–15	Right Arm	8/4
16–18	Left Arm	8/4
19–20	Head	8/5

Combat Style: Firearms 69%

Weapon	Size/Force	Damage	AP/HP
AK-774	H	2d6	Vacc Rated Assault Rifle

Marine Jones (Tech)

Jones is a practical joker, always playing sophomoric tricks on his fellow marines. He once smuggled a tub of cockroaches on board, which backfired when the insects escaped and laid eggs in the life support air scrubbers, taking him a week to clean by hand. Despite his annoying pranks, Jones is easily kept in line due to an almost paranoid level of superstition.

Jones	Attributes
STR: 11	Action Points: 2 (3)
CON: 11	Damage Modifier: +1d2
SIZ: 16	Movement: 6 metres
DEX: 13	Initiative Bonus: +15 (+9 in Armour)
INT: 17	Armour: Marine Vacc Suit
POW: 15	
CHA: 11	

Standard Skills
Athletics 57%, Brawn 37%, Conceal 55%, Customs 54%, Dance 42%, Deceit 64%, Drive 45%, Endurance 60%, Evade 59%, First Aid 37%, Influence 41%, Insight 36%, Locale 52%, Perception 48%, Stealth 40%, Unarmed 80%, Willpower 55%

Professional Skills
Computers 91%, Electronics 86%, EVA 58%, Gambling 66%, Lockpicking 75%, Lore (Squad Tactics) 41%, Mechanics 56%, Navigation 42%, Sensors 57%, Streetwise 41%, Survival (Planetary) 42%, Survival (Space) 68%

Passions
Hate EVA 75%, Superstitious 78%, Loyalty to UNSN 54%

1d20	Location	AP/HP
01–03	Right Leg	8/6
04–16	Left Leg	8/6
07–09	Abdomen	8/7
10–12	Chest	8/8
13–15	Right Arm	8/5
16–18	Left Arm	8/5
19–20	Head	8/6

Combat Style: Firearms 70%

Weapon	Size/Force	Damage	AP/HP
AK-774	H	2d6	Vacc Rated Assault Rifle

Marine Moreau (Assault)

Moreau is an earnest marine, always willing to do his best despite the shit jobs he ends up receiving. His major flaws are an almost pathological hatred of insects (having once had several cockroaches trapped in his suit during an EVA) combined with a very itchy trigger finger. Other than that, he is good natured and always reminisces about his country upbringing on Earth.

Moreau	Attributes
STR: 14	Action Points: 2 (3)
CON: 13	Damage Modifier: +1d2
SIZ: 14	Movement: 6 metres
DEX: 13	Initiative Bonus: +14 (+8 in Armour)
INT: 14	Armour: Marine Vacc Suit
POW: 11	
CHA: 15	

Standard Skills
Athletics 55%, Brawn 56%, Conceal 39%, Customs 51%, Dance 46%, Deceit 41%, Drive 63%, Endurance 65%, Evade 66%, First Aid 37%, Influence 36%, Insight 50%, Locale 59%, Perception 61%, Stealth 57%, Unarmed 75%, Willpower 60%

Professional Skills
Comms 41%, Demolitions 75%, EVA 57%, Gambling 48%, Lore (Squad Tactics) 40%, Navigation 42%, Sensors 59%, Streetwise 63%, Survival (Planetary) 40%, Survival (Space) 64%

Passions
Hate Bugs 81%, Trigger Happy 61%, Loyalty to UNSN 88%

1d20	Location	AP/HP
01–03	Right Leg	8/6
04–16	Left Leg	8/6
07–09	Abdomen	8/7
10–12	Chest	8/8
13–15	Right Arm	8/5
16–18	Left Arm	8/5
19–20	Head	8/6

Combat Style: Blades 69%, Firearms 73%, Heavy Weapons 81%

Weapon	Size/Force	Damage	AP/HP
Combat Knife	S	1d4+1+1d2	6/8
AK-774	H	2d6	Vacc Rated Assault Rifle

Marine Mumba (Assault)

Mumba has an insubordinate attitude. He talks-back constantly, although his behaviour changes in combat situations where he proves to be ruthlessly effective, following orders to the letter. Due to this he ends up having to do most of the scutwork as punishment duty, but puts up with it for the chance to serve in combat environments.

Mumba	Attributes
STR: 16	Action Points: 2 (3)
CON: 11	Damage Modifier: +1d4
SIZ: 15	Movement: 6 metres
DEX: 18	Initiative Bonus: +15 (+9 in Armour)
INT: 12	Armour: Marine Vacc Suit
POW: 11	
CHA: 8	

Standard Skills
Athletics 62%, Brawn 83%, Conceal 45%, Customs 60%, Dance 54%, Deceit 45%, Drive 54%, Endurance 78%, Evade 53%, First Aid 39%, Influence 41%, Insight 40%, Locale 58%, Perception 56%, Stealth 72%, Unarmed 57%, Willpower 55%

Professional Skills
Comms 46%, Demolitions 65%, EVA 59%, Gambling 42%, Lore (Squad Tactics) 36%, Navigation 57%, Sensors 36%, Streetwise 61%, Survival (Planetary) 52%, Survival (Space) 58%

Passions
See Conspiracy Theories 74%, Be Insubordinate 89%, Loyalty to UNSN 53%

1d20	Location	AP/HP
01–03	Right Leg	8/6
04–16	Left Leg	8/6
07–09	Abdomen	8/7
10–12	Chest	8/8
13–15	Right Arm	8/5
16–18	Left Arm	8/5
19–20	Head	8/6

Combat Style: Blades 83%, Firearms 74%, Heavy Weapons 67%

Weapon	Size/Force	Damage	AP/HP
Combat Knife	S	1d4+1+1d4	6/8
AK-774	H	2d6	Vacc Rated Assault Rifle

Marine Vladimir (Gunner)

A fearless marine, Vladimir prefers using big guns to anything personal firearms. The quad strafing lasers on the assault shuttle; the Nergal's 50mm gauss cannon; indeed anything you have to sit in an accelerator couch or turret to fire. If not performing targeting exercises, he spends his time lovingly servicing the death dealing devices.

Vladimir	Attributes
STR: 17	Action Points: 3
CON: 14	Damage Modifier: +1d4
SIZ: 17	Movement: 6 metres
DEX: 13	Initiative Bonus: +13 (+7 in Armour)
INT: 13	Armour: Marine Vacc Suit
POW: 9	
CHA: 9	

Standard Skills
Athletics 47%, Boating 44%, Brawn 82%, Conceal 49%, Customs 51%, Dance 39%, Deceit 41%, Drive 41%, Endurance 60%, Evade 61%, First Aid 43%, Influence 36%, Insight 56%, Locale 50%, Perception 76%, Ride 41%, Sing 33%, Stealth 51%, Swim 40%, Unarmed 79%, Willpower 54%

Professional Skills
Craft (Machinist) 72%, Electronics 50%, EVA 77%, Lore (Squad Tactics) 35%, Mechanics 63%, Navigation 44%, Sensors 50%, Streetwise 41%, Survival (Planetary) 55%, Survival (Space) 59%

Passions
Love Big Guns 73%, Act Fearlessly 76%, Loyalty to UNSN 58%

1d20	Location	AP/HP
01–03	Right Leg	8/7
04–16	Left Leg	8/7
07–09	Abdomen	8/8
10–12	Chest	8/9
13–15	Right Arm	8/6
16–18	Left Arm	8/6
19–20	Head	8/7

Combat Style (Firearms) 71%, Combat Style (Gunnery) 83%

Weapon	Size/Force	Damage	AP/HP
AK-774	H	2d6	Vacc Rated Assault Rifle

M-Space Ship Statistics

UNCC Nergal

Tartarus Class, UN Customs Cutter
Length 63m, Width 15m

SPEED: 6 (9 Engine Modules @ TR70)
HANDLING: 2 (3 Maneuver Modules @ TR70)
SIZE: 102

Modules:
Bridge 2
Mainframe 1
Captain's Stateroom 4
Staterooms 14
Crew Mess 15
Hibernation Chamber 15
Weapons 2+2+2+10=16
Life Support 5
Power Plant 12 (TR70)
Shuttle Bay 20

Armor 1
Shields –
Stealth -10%
Hyperspace: 0.14

Weapons:
Spinal Rail Cannon 2d6
Pulse Laser (x2) 1d6
Missiles (8) 3d6

Shuttle (10 Modules):
Cockpit 1, Passengers 8, Engine+Maneuver 1 (TR40)

Speed 2, Handling 2, Size 10

DCV Fukunusubi

Titan Class Salvage Ship
Length 195m, Width 95m

SPEED: 3 (30 Engine Modules @ TR30)
HANDLING: 1 (10 Maneuver Modules @ TR30)
SIZE: 267

Modules:
Bridge 3
Mainframe 2
Captain's Stateroom 4
Staterooms 24
Crew Mess 16
Hibernation Chamber 30
Locker Room 13
Ship's Stores 15
Manufactory Bay 40
Repair Bay 40
Life Support 40
Power Plant 40 (TR 30)

Armor –
Shields –

Stealth –

Hyperspace: 0.1

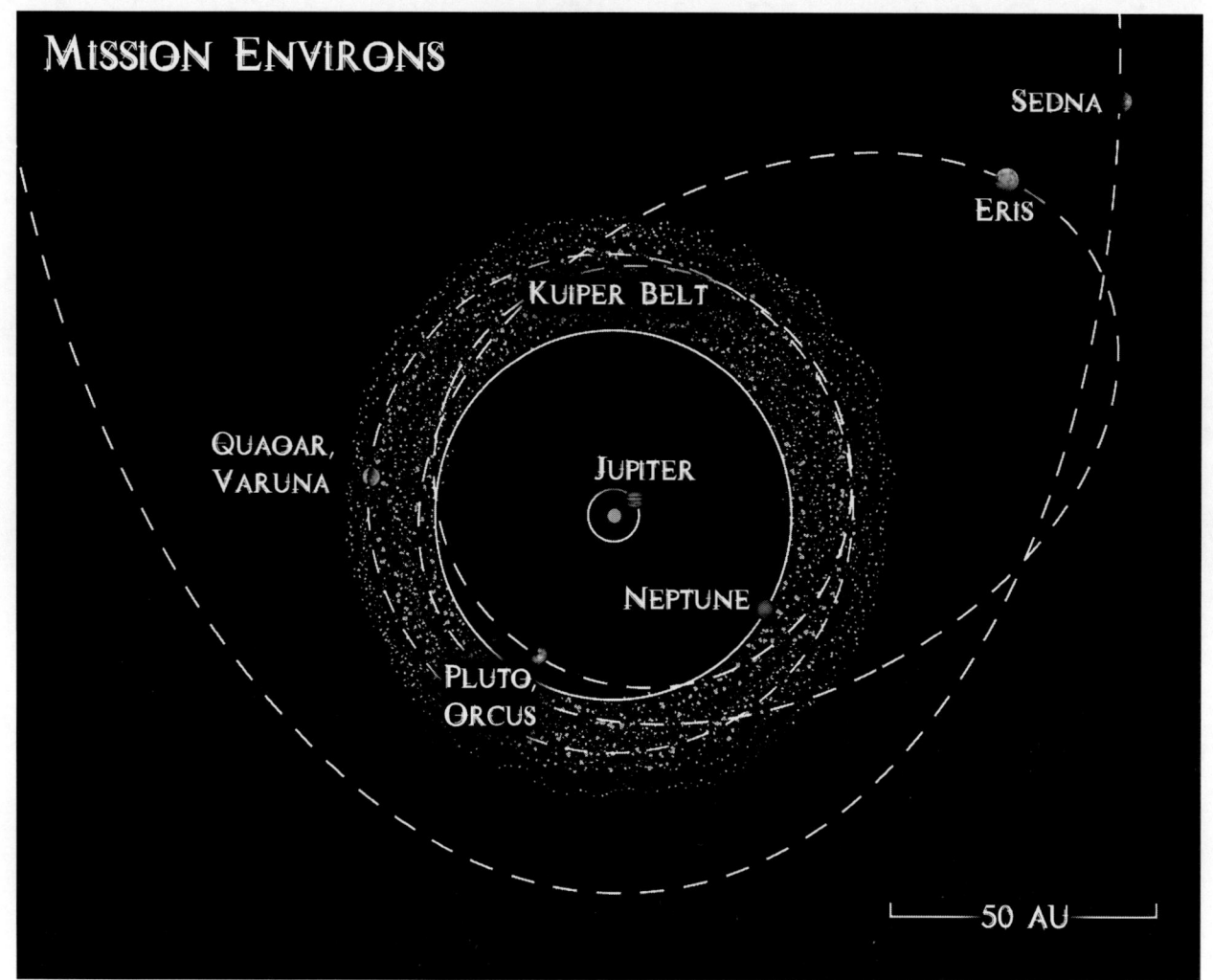

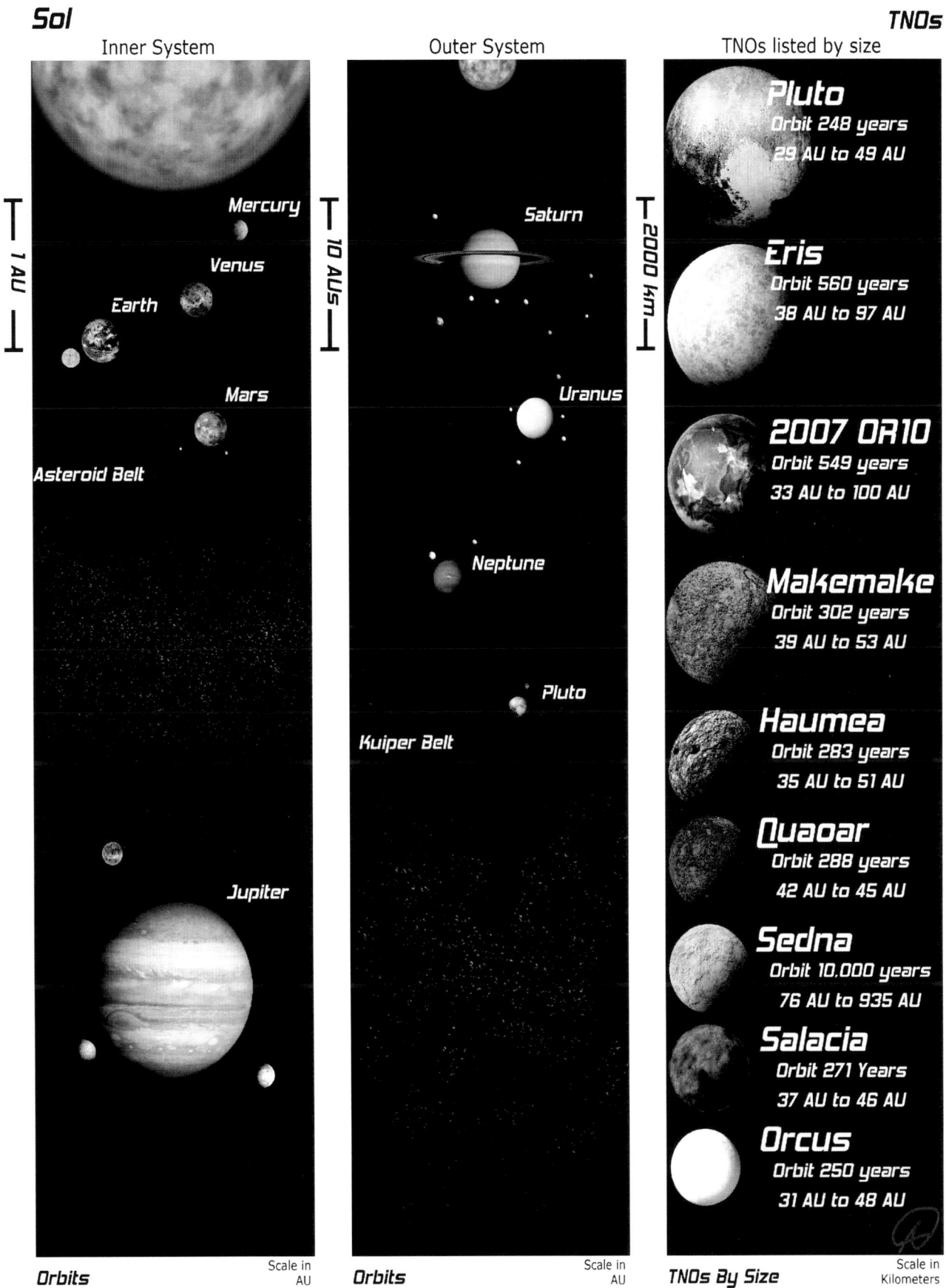

Trans-Neptunian Objects

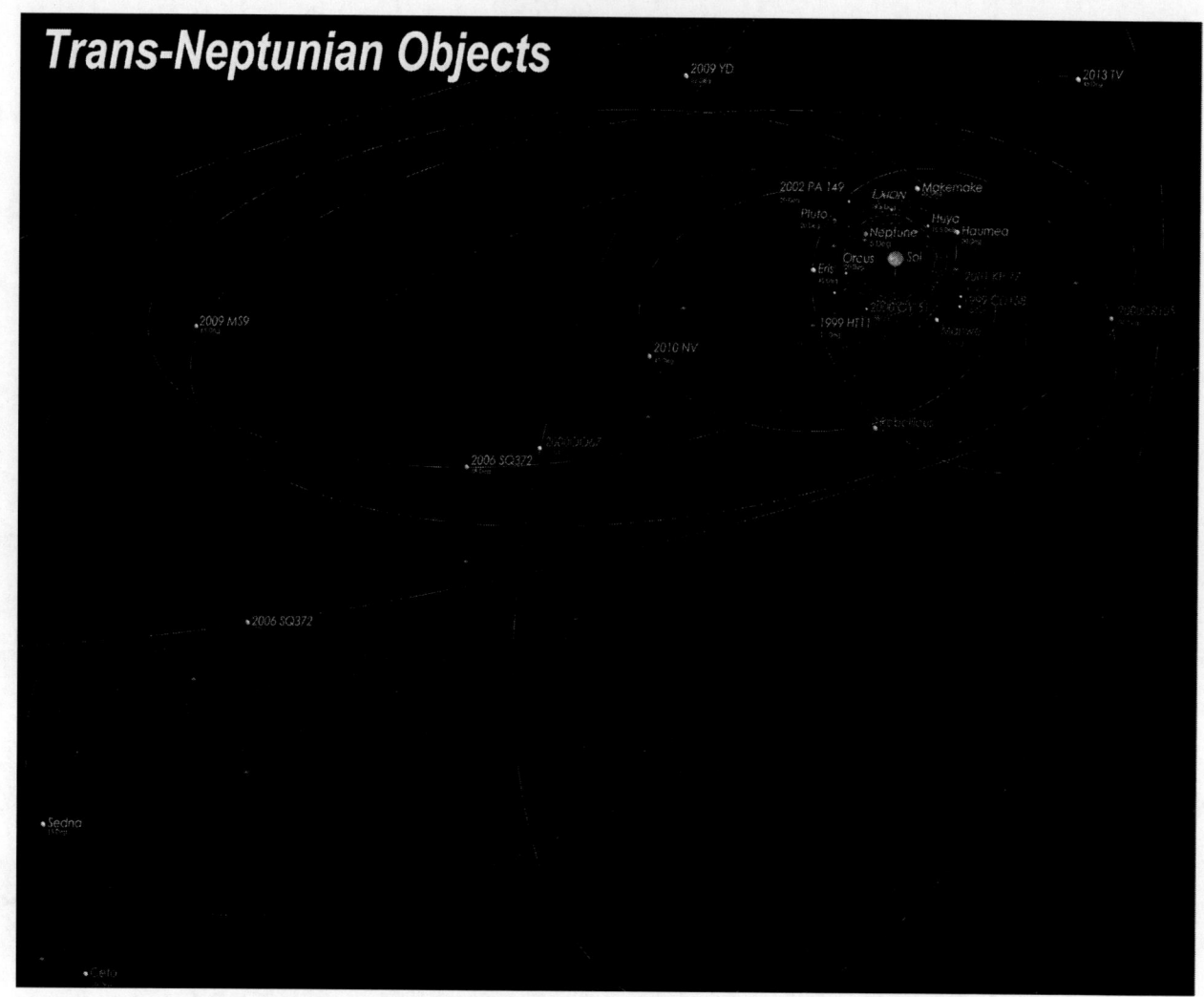